CAN RGUsON

From schoolboy star to making grade at Ibrox

DUNCAN'S STORY: PART I

DUNCAN FERGUSON was born on December 27th, 1971 in Stirling, Scotland.

Today, Stirling is Scotland's youngest city gaining the status in the summer of 2002. It is Scotland's heritage capital, where the Wars of Independence were fought and won and where, for three centuries, monarchs ruled in regal splendour while merchants and craftsmen plied their trade below the castle rock.

Stirling's sense of history still surrounds the area, typified by the landmark cliff-top castle in the Old Town.

Three weeks before Duncan came into the world, East Pakistan was established as the independent country of East Pakistan.

By the time of his birth, A Clockwork Orange was the leading new release at the cinemas, while musically (!), Benny Hill topped the singles charts with Ernie (The Fastest Milkman In The West) and Andy Williams's Greatest Hits (the original version) held the number one slot in the album charts.

Duncan had his eye on a career in football from an early age.

Local hero: Dunc (circled) in his school team and (above) his school building in Stirling

Stirling had already produced Leeds United midfield general Billy Bremner and the young Ferguson started kicking a ball about at his family's flat in Graystale Road, St Ninians and later, around the corner at the new family home off Baillie Waugh Road.

These were the venues that provided the backdrop to Duncan's dreams of soccer stardom.

It was at Bannockburn High School - a 10-minute walk from the home he shared with his parents and two sisters - that he started playing organised football.

A strong sporting ethos dominated at the imposing red-brick school, clearly indicated by the numerous football, rugby and hockey pitches that surround the main building. ❯

Rangers fan Duncan was snapped up by the local ICI side at the age of 12 and began to establish a reputation as a brave centre-forward.

A move to Carse Thistle followed where manager Dick Taylor was always impressed by the youngster's dedication.

Speaking to The Evertonian in 1998, he explained: "Duncan had been with a couple of clubs before he came to us but we were looking for a striker and we found Duncan.

"He stayed with us for three years until he was 15. He went to Bannockburn High School, with a lot of the other boys and they gave him rave reviews.

"Duncan always wanted to be a footballer and he was a good trainer.

"His dad, Duncan, was more interested than a lot of the other dads and he was very keen on his son's career."

Taylor stressed that Ferguson's aerial abilities were there to see from an early age. He exploited this facet of his game in the Scottish Central Boys' League.

"We had a bit of a secret weapon in those days with Duncan, although there were probably five at the time who were as good as him.

"The thing is, they weren't as dedicated as Duncan and they didn't have dads who wanted them to be professional footballers."

George Skelton was the scout who spotted Duncan's potential in 1985 and marked him down as one to watch after seeing him score four times in a 6-0 win.

He told The Evertonian: "I saw him in a Stirling boys' team, Carse Thistle, after he had actually scored 100 goals in one season for ICI.

"They were the best team in the area, but then Duncan moved over to Carse Thistle and scored over 100 goals - again in one season.

"I approached the manager, Dick Taylor, and he allowed me to get him into training for Dundee United boys at Stirling University.

"Then I put him in a trial match and he was absolutely superb. He was out on the right-hand byline and he flicked the ball with his right leg, inside his left leg, turned around and thrashed it home.

"Then we knew we had to get the boy signed."

Duncan accompanied his father, Duncan senior, to Tannadice to sign schoolboy forms.

He was eventually offered a two-year apprenticeship and signed full-time terms with the Tangerines in 1990 after netting four goals in a reserve game against Aberdeen.

As a kid he was always getting forward in the six-yard box and scored an

Rising star: In action at Tannadice (top) and signing in at Rangers

'When he lined-up for a game against Raith Rovers in April 1994, he could have had little idea about the impact one incident would have on his career and his life'

enormous number of goals," added George.

"And within a couple of years, he developed fantastic timing in the air. He was only a tiny wee boy when I first saw him, but a year later he had grown about six inches.

"He had this tremendous ability to hang in the air and when I saw him first of all, I thought: 'This boy will be a bit special.'

But Duncan had to wait patiently to make his impression.

"In our coaching sessions, I thought he was a bit shy and thought I might have made a mistake," admitted George.

"But it became clear that I hadn't.

"He was a great lad and the bother he has suffered wasn't really his fault - he just stands up to people.

George soon had a good idea Duncan would make it at the highest level.

"When he scored that special goal in the trial match I knew he was going to play for Scotland.

"He was one of the most special players I had ever found."

Duncan achieved a childhood dream when he made his professional debut at Ibrox, home of his boyhood favourites Rangers on November 11, 1990. He even finished on the winning side as Dundee United recorded a 2-1 win. By the end of that season, he had established himself as a regular in Jim McLean's starting line-up, making nine appearances and scoring one league goal.

It was in the Scottish Cup, however, that he really started to make his mark.

He netted three times in five ties as Dundee United reached the 1991 final, although they were pipped 4-3 after extra time by Motherwell in the showpiece event.

Duncan finished the next two seasons as top scorer at Tannadice and earned his first call-up to the national team in 1992. He won his first cap as a substitute against the United States and won selection for further internationals against Canada, Holland and Germany by the end of 1993.

Duncan had something of a confrontational relationship with manager McLean and his chairman. The Tangerines had already turned down £3m bids from Bayern Munich, Leeds and Chelsea and Everton were also among his suitors even then.

In June 1993, the Liverpool Echo carried a back page splash about Howard Kendall having a bid rejected.

Kendall revealed: "With the permission of my chairman, I made a very big offer which was turned down.

"The offer was topped by Leeds who

Turning point: That controversial incident with Raith Rovers' defender
John McStay in 1994. Right: With Rangers boss Walter Smith and (below)
with Ibrox team-mates Andy Goram and Ally McCoist

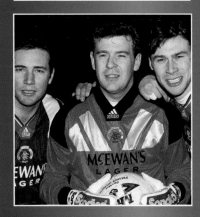

were given permission to talk to the player. Naturally I'd like to be in a position to match Leeds and give him another choice.

"He's a player we've been chasing for a while, but whether we are in a position to increase our offer is something which will have to be discussed by the chairman."

In the event, Ferguson stayed put until later that year when McLean's successor - former Southampton full-back Ivan Golac - agreed to sell him to Rangers for a then British record fee of £4million.

The move was not welcomed by the majority of Dundee United fans although the windfall helped fund the redevelopment of Tannadice.

Walter Smith was the man responsible for breaking the British transfer record to get his man.

Smith had started his managerial career at Dundee United under McLean, just as Ferguson had broken onto the first-team scene.

There was a huge weight of expectation on Duncan's shoulders at Ibrox but a series of injury problems restricted his appearances for the Light Blues.

But when he lined-up for a game against Raith Rovers in April 1994, he could have had little idea about the impact one incident would have on his career and his life.

Ferguson was charged with assault after the authorities reviewed video footage of an altercation with Raith defender John McStay.

To add to his woes, the Scottish FA imposed a 12-match playing ban for the same offence - a punishment put on hold pending Ferguson's appeal.

After only 14 games and two goals for the Gers, Duncan agreed to a fresh start and agreed to head south to join Everton on loan, along with Rangers colleague Ian Durrant.

It signalled a move away from the goldfish bowl of Glasgow and 'Fergie' was soon hitting the headlines for all the right reasons on Merseyside.

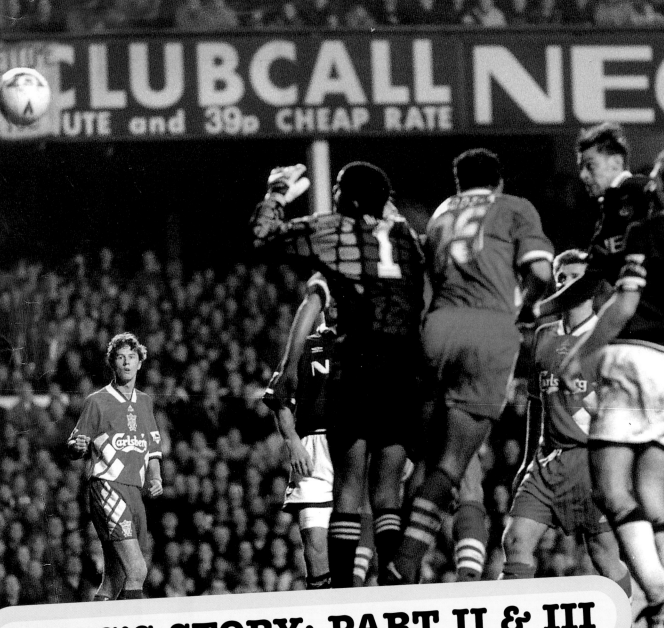

DUNC'S STORY: PART II & III

DUNCAN may have been a little reticent about a move to England in the first place, but within weeks he knew he had made the right decision.

Ironically it was Mike Walker who had brought him to Goodison along with Rangers team-mate Ian Durrant but the former Norwich boss was on borrowed time irrespective of his moves into the loan market.

Joe Royle replaced him and, knowing exactly what it took to be an Everton number nine, struck up a good rapport with the big Scot.

Joe's first game in charge provided the perfect setting for both of them - a Merseyside derby at Goodison.

It was November 21st, 1994 and a buoyant Goodison saw Royle's first night nerves dispelled by Duncan's first goal verve. The second half was 11 minutes old when Andy Hinchcliffe swung in a corner and Fergie placed a deft header past David James for his opening goal in Everton colours as the Blues defeated their rivals 2-0.

When Duncan headed an almost identical goal in a win against Leeds a fortnight later, Everton were off the bottom and Fergie-mania began to take hold.

Choruses of 'Don't Go Back To Rangers' regularly reverberated around Goodison and Royle famously remarked: 'Duncan became a legend before he became a player at Everton.'

The Blues stuck by their man over his looming court case and underlined the faith they had in the new crowd favourite by making moves to make his switch from Rangers permanent.

The Everton club merchandise stalls went into overdrive with Fergie t-shirts and related products flying off the hangers.

By now, Ferguson had come to the conclusion that his future lay on Merseyside and he indicated that he would be willing to agree to a long-term switch.

The birth of Dunc mania

ON December 13th, 1994, Everton fans received the Christmas present they all wanted.

Duncan put pen to paper on a four-and-a-half year deal after a £4m fee was finally agreed with Rangers.

Everton captain Dave Watson summed up the news when he said: "We haven't really had a superstar here for a long time - someone who the fans really look up to.

"But Duncan is the man for the job. He is a legend. It is Fergiemania!"

Manager Joe Royle was not surprised by Watson's verdict.

"I know the players will be delighted with the news of the signing. They have come to like Duncan a lot. He has a great spirit and a driving will to win. It is important that my first signing was a big one and a good one.

"Duncan has immense potential. He is also a terrific lad who is still only 22 and ready to go on learning. The fans have taken to him. That is easy to see. In the short time he has been here, he has played his full part in our mini-revival."

As the new year arrived, Duncan prepared to hear his fate from the courts but had his hearing adjourned until May. The dozen-match playing ban the Scottish FA wanted to impose for the same offence, was also postponed until the same time freeing Fergie to concentrate on helping the Blues beat the drop.

January saw the first of his eight sendings-off for the Blues. It came after he pushed John Jensen in the chest and the Gunners' Dane fell to the ground holding his face and Darlington official Robbie Hart deemed it to be a red card offence. The ensuing suspension ruled him out of the derby return at Anfield but Duncan was back in the line-up for the February visit of Manchester United to Goodison.

By now, Duncan could do little wrong in the eyes of Evertonians and he added to his status by netting the only goal of the game as the Blues defeated the champions.

Like his big-game winner against Liverpool three months earlier, it came from a header following a Hinchcliffe corner. He celebrated by taking his shirt off and twirling it around his head while giving fans his trademark clenched-fist salute.

This brought censure from the English FA who deemed the celebrations 'over-excessive.'

The next twist in an eventful first season at Goodison came in March when he was sent-off again after a clash with Leicester's Jimmy Willis at Filbert Street.

Video evidence suggested Ferguson's innocence as did Willis and some of his Leicester team-mates but match referee Paul Durkin refused to review his decision and the suspension ruled the big centre-forward out of the Blues' epic FA Cup semi-final defeat of Spurs at Elland Road.

A miserable month was completed when Duncan was fined £500 and banned from driving for a year after giving a positive breath test for drink-driving.

To compound matters, Duncan then broke down in this comeback game at Sheffield Wednesday and it was revealed he required a double hernia operation - making him doubtful for the FA Cup final showdown with Manchester United.

In the meantime, Everton won their battle against relegation with a game to spare thanks to a 1-0 win at Ipswich and Duncan stepped up his bid to prove his fitness ahead of the Blues' date at Wembley.

He later admitted: "The turning point for me came even after only a couple of weeks. I liked the city, I liked the fans and the players were great. It didn't go too well for me at Rangers because they had a class striker up there in Mark Hateley who was battering in the goals.

"I had to sit on the touchline because he was a quality striker. He was number one and I was number two. Now I'm playing regular first team football and feeling the benefits of it. Everton's fans are renowned for their hospitality as are the people of Liverpool and they have taken to me - long may it continue."

'Everton's fans are renowned for their hospitality as are the people of Liverpool and they have taken to me - long may it continue'

HE spoke about the
atmosphere of
Goodison, the history
of the club, the
passion of the fans
and his burning
desire to follow in the
illustrious footsteps
of those legendary
number nines that
had gone before him.
He would turn out to
be a man of few
words who preferred
to let his actions do
the talking but from
one of his early
interviews, it became
clear that Duncan
and Everton were a
match made in
heaven . . .

'I loved it as soon as I came. I knew that this was a big club and I was confident that I could settle here easily. The people of Everton were brilliant'

DUNCAN EXCLUSIVE

First love: Signing on loan with Ian Durrant, a vital goal against Leeds to ease relegation fears in 1995 and (top) with a print that showed the fans were already taking him to their hearts

D UNCAN FERGUSON spoke exclusively to The Evertonian magazine about why he opted for a big money move to Goodison Park.

The Scotland striker, who quickly became something of a cult figure among the Everton fans, was an instant hit when Mike Walker took him on loan in October, 1994. And Joe Royle was so impressed with the 6ft 3ins centre-forward that he completed what was Britain's second best transfer at the time to keep him at Everton permanently.

It was a move which never looked likely when Ferguson first arrived at Goodison because Rangers boss Walter Smith was reluctant to sell Big Dunc. But Fergie soon found his feet at Bellefield and quickly became one of the the most popular players in the Everton dressing room.

Duncan said: "Joe had a big influence on me coming to the club because he was a striker and he wanted both him and the club, to be successful. He pointed out, too, that he wanted me and the fans have been absolutely brilliant. They will now see the best of me when I settle down and now that I'm an official Evertonian."

Duncan was cleared to play for Everton for most of the rest of the season when the court case over his alleged headbutt offence was adjourned until May 9.

"Before, of course, I was just on loan and at first I just thought I would be here for three months," said Duncan, who has just turned 23.

'I wasn't aware of the history surrounding the place. Now I know about the long line of great number nines and hopefully, I can continue their reputation'

"Rangers pointed out to me that I would be back and that was as far as I was thinking ahead. I was disappointed to be going out on loan, but once I was into it with Everton it wasn't a wrench to leave Rangers." Duncan soon wanted to become a permanent Everton player, along with Rangers team-mate Ian Durrant. But while Ian returned to Ibrox, Duncan was more than pleased to stay.

"I loved it as soon as I came," he said. "It didn't take me long to settle in after the first week or two. I knew that this was a big club and I was confident that I could settle here easily. The people of Everton and the city of Liverpool have been great to me, the fans have been brilliant and everything's ticking along nicely.

"I didn't need to leave Rangers if I didn't want to, but I liked everything about Everton and it was an easy decision for me.

"It was also good that the team started to win but I always knew that things would improve for this team anyway.

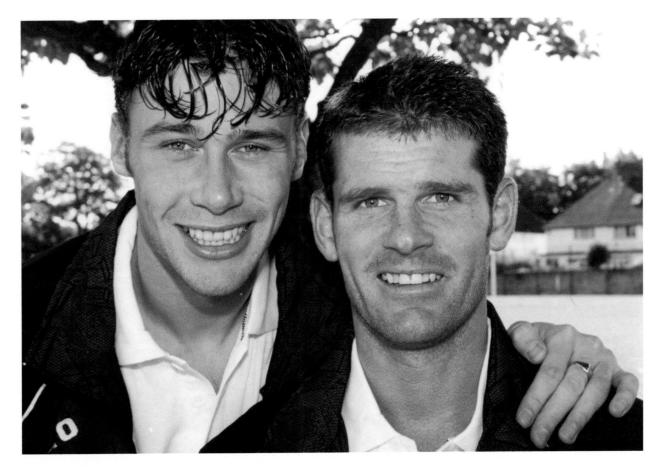

"We are on the way up and I knew that we would climb the league if the team worked hard."

The passionate atmosphere at Goodison Park was another factor which persuaded Duncan to move south to Everton.

"The atmosphere was good at Ibrox," said Fergie. "But, in fact, the atmosphere at Goodison is better because at Ibrox some of the fans are set in their ways about winning and they expect it, which takes the buzz out.

"But the Everton fans are all fired up to help get the team out of the relegation scene. The gates have been exceptional . . .even in midweek. It's a lot of money to go to football nowadays, so it shows how much passion there is for the club."

He added: "I always knew Everton was no small club, but I wasn't that aware of the history surrounding the place. Now I know about the long line of great number nines they have had here and, hopefully, I can continue their reputation in some way.

"But I'm not an Andy Gray or a Graeme Sharp...I'm Duncan Ferguson. They have been very successful at this club and, obviously I now want to be just as successful.

"The club have shovelled out a lot of money for me. Hopefully I can repay some of that with some good performances and the team will keep winning."

Dunc, who was targeted by Howard Kendall in 1993, continued: "I know what we won in the eighties, but now we are trying to avoid going down, so we must work hard to keep ourselves up. Then we will think about winning trophies."

Turning to his own style of play, Fergie warned fans: "I have not really been known as a great

goalscorer! There's a lot to my game and I never set goalscoring targets - except for the whole team. It doesn't matter if the keeper scores goals, as long as we move up the table. Everybody must work hard together and Willie Donachie has been getting us to do just that. He knows his football and combined with the gaffer, the two of them make a good partnership."

Big Dunc was determined not to let two £4m price tags become millstones around his neck and he did not feel the pressure of being one of Britain's most valuable players.

"One way I see it, a club could pay £10m for me and it would still be nothing to do with me," he said. "It doesn't put any extra pressure on. I'm still the same player that I was."

After helping the team clear of a relegation threat in his first season, Duncan was dealt an off-the-pitch blow 10 days before the FA Cup final, which the Blues had reached for the first time in six years after a thrilling defeat of Spurs.

He was found guilty of assault with sentencing deferred until after the final. The English FA also confirmed their plans to invoke the Scottish FA's 12-game ban should that decision be upheld.

On a happier note, Fergie recovered from injury to take his place on the bench for the final against hot favourites Manchester United. The solitary winning goal in a surprise victory came from one of Duncan's strike partners Paul Rideout, Fergie replacing the goalscorer for the final half-hour.

His blue nose picture was to become a famous image and Fergie later donned his kilt for the evening's celebrations, capping off a memorable first season at his new club.

Double Scots: New boys Ian Durrant and Duncan Ferguson pose for a photo on arriving at Bellefield in 1994

Deadly
DUNC

6

DUNCAN opened his
account in the best
possible way for
Evertonians - with a
strike against
Liverpool. Among his
early goalkeeping
victims was also a
certain Nigel Martyn.
In part one of the
Ferguson goal story, we
relive the magic from
1994 to 1998 . . .

1994-95

Goal 1. 21/11/94. Everton 2 (Ferguson, Rideout) Liverpool 0.
The beginning of the legend. Duncan rises expertly to place a deft header past David James from Andy Hinchcliffe's corner and set the Royle era off to a winning start.

Goal 2. 5/12/94. Everton 3 (Rideout, Ferguson, Unsworth) Leeds United 0.
Another Hinchcliffe cross met by a bullet header which flew past John Lukic.

Goal 3. 26/12/94. Everton 1 (Ferguson) Sheffield Wednesday 4.
A towering header from a David Burrows cross which actually put the Blues 1-0 up.

Goal 4. 31/12/94. Everton 4 (Ferguson, Rideout 2, Watson) Ipswich Town 1.
A close range equaliser in front of the Gwladys Street.

Goals 5 and 6. 21/01/95. Everton 3 (Ferguson 2, Rideout) Crystal Palace 1.
A two-goal salvo past Nigel Martyn. The first was a powerful header back across the goalkeeper from an Andy Hinchcliffe cross; the second a low left-footed strike.

Goal 7. FA Cup. 18/02/95. Everton 5 (Limpar, Parkinson, Rideout, Ferguson, Stuart) Norwich City 0.
Anders Limpar's astute pass sent Ferguson racing away through the middle for number four.

Goal 8. 25/02/95. Everton 1 (Ferguson) Manchester United 0.
A classic match-winner. Hinchcliffe supplied the corner, Duncan the header past Peter Schmeichel and before you knew it, the shirt was off as Ferguson embarked on his trademark celebration.

1994-95: Premiership: 22+1 apps, 7 goals. Cups 4+1 apps, 1 goal. Total: 26+2 apps, 8 goals.

1995-96

Goals 9 and 10. 01/01/96. Wimbledon 2 Everton 3 (Ebbrell, Ferguson 2).
Two goals in three minutes put Everton ›

3-0 up and gave Duncan the perfect start to the new year.

After 25 minutes, he hit a fine swivelling volley - his first goal away from Goodison Park. A few minutes later, he swept in a cross from David Unsworth.

Goal 11. FA Cup. 17/01/96. Stockport County 2 Everton 3 (Stuart, Ferguson, Ebbrell).

Graham Stuart whipped the corner over and Duncan powered his header home from about four yards before running over to the travelling Evertonians where he was duly mobbed.

Goal 12. FA Cup. 27/01/96. Everton 2 (Amokachi, Ferguson) Port Vale 2.

When Duncan struck with just two minutes to go, it looked like the Blues were through to the next round but a late leveller paved the way for Vale to spring a shock in the replay. Anders Limpar sent in a routine cross but goalkeeper Paul Musselwhite spilled it at Duncan's feet and he did the rest.

Goal 13. 24/02/96. Everton 3 (Kanchelskis, Watson, Ferguson) Nottingham Forest 0.

A classic headed goal. Andrei Kanchelskis provided the cross and Ferguson charged in to bury it past Mark Crossley.

Goals 14 and 15. 09/03/96. Everton 2 (Ferguson 2) Coventry City 2.

Everton had gone into the lead when Ferguson rose above defender David Busst to head in a cross from Graham Stuart. The formidable frontman also got Everton's second with a charge through the middle, brushing Busst and Liam Daish aside, before steering his shot beyond Steve Ogrizovic.

1995-96: Premiership: 16+2 apps, 5 goals. Cups 2 apps, 2 goals. Total: 18+2 apps, 7 goals.

1996-97

Goals 16 and 17. 21/08/96. Manchester United 2 Everton 2 (Ferguson 2).

Big Dunc always relished a trip to Old Trafford and he silenced the home faithful by bagging a brace.

His breathtaking opener came after he received a pass from United old boy Andrei Kanchelskis on the edge of the area, turned and drilled a ferocious rising shot past Peter Schmeichel.

Six minutes later he rose at the far post to bury Andy Hinchcliffe's inviting first-time centre.

Goal 18. 30/11/96. Everton 1 (Ferguson) Sunderland 3.
An outstanding goal after coming off the bench, heading in the equaliser from a Nick Barmby cross. But two late Michael Bridges goals won it for the visitors.

Goal 19. 26/12/96. Middlesbrough 4 Everton 2 (Unsworth, Ferguson).
Nick Barmby threatened to spoil the Middlesbrough party on his first game at the Riverside since his move to Everton when he provided the cross for Ferguson to head home and make it 2-2 on the stroke of half-time. Again, it wasn't enough as two second-half goals from Juninho won it.

Goal 20. 05/01/97. Everton 3 (Kanchelskis, Barmby, Ferguson) Swindon Town 0.
Duncan claimed the Blues' third goal five minutes into the second half with a fine header from Earl Barrett's cross.

Goal 21. 11/01/97. Sheffield Wednesday 2 Everton 1 (Ferguson).
Michael Branch sent over a pinpoint cross and Ferguson managed to direct his header past Kevin Pressman from six yards.

Goal 22. 19/01/97. Arsenal 3 Everton 1 (Ferguson).
A late headed consolation goal from Nick Barmby's corner.

Goal 23. 01/02/97. Everton 2 (Ferguson, Barmby) Nottingham Forest 0.
Duncan takes the ball around Colin Cooper and Mark Crossley before slamming a shot into the Gwladys Street goal.

Goal 24. 05/03/97. Southampton 2 Everton 2 (Ferguson, Speed).
A bizarre opening goal when a header from the edge of the area seemed to lack power but bounced up past Maik Taylor and into the net.

Goal 25. 16/04/97. Everton 1 (Ferguson) Liverpool 1.
Dunc serves up his derby best again, wheeling to fire a fierce drive past David James for a 65th minute equaliser.

Goal 26. 19/04/97. West Ham 2 Everton 2 (Branch, Ferguson).
Duncan nets the equaliser three minutes into stoppage time to give the Blues a

vital point in their bid for Premiership survival.

He swept home a Barmby cross to send the visiting Evertonians into ecstasy.

1996-97: Premiership: 31+2 apps, 10 goals. Cups 3 apps, 1 goal. Total: 34+2 apps, 11 goals.

1997-98

Goal 27. 09/08/97. Everton 1 (Ferguson) Crystal Palace 2.
The big Scot headed home with five minutes to go, but it proved too little too late for the Blues.

Goal 28. 08/11/97. Blackburn Rovers 3 Everton 2 (Speed, Ferguson).
A close range finish after good work on the left by John Oster.

Goals 29, 30 and 31. 28/12/97. Everton 3 (Ferguson 3) Bolton Wanderers 2.
Duncan's only hat-trick for Everton as he returned from a three-match ban to net three headers on a day when he proved too hot to handle.

Wearing the captain's armband, he was at his most hungry and scored his first with a soaring header past Gavin Ward from Tony Thomas's cross from the right.

Barmby provided the assist for the second with Duncan diving to steer home his header.

He completed his hat-trick midway through the second period when another Thomas cross was powered past Ward.

Goal 32. 10/01/98. Crystal Palace 1 Everton 3 (Barmby, Ferguson, Madar).
Ferguson heads in the Blues' second with the Palace defence rooted to the spot.

Goal 33. 18/01/98. Everton 3 (Speed, Ferguson, OG) Chelsea 1.
Barmby's corner is headed home for Duncan's fifth goal in three games.

Goal 34. 07/02/98. Barnsley 2 Everton 2 (Ferguson, Grant).
Skipper Duncan starts and finishes the move, linking up with Mickael Madar and Mitch Ward, before stooping to head home Mark Ward's cross.

Goal 35. 21/02/98. Liverpool 1 Everton 1 (Ferguson).
Michael Ball's throw is knocked back for Ferguson to drive beyond David James from the edge of the box.

Goal 36. 11/04/98. Everton 2 (Hinchcliffe, Ferguson) Leeds United 0.
Robert Molenaar conceded a free-kick, John O'Kane lifted the ball into the box and Ferguson powered home Everton's second.

Goal 37. 25/04/98. Everton 1 (Ferguson) Sheffield Wednesday 3.
Duncan nods the ball past Kevin Pressman after Slaven Bilic had hoisted a high ball into the box.

1997-98: Premiership: 28+1 apps, 11 goals. Cups 3 apps, 0 goals. Total: 31+1 apps, 11 goals.

1998-99

Goals 38 and 39. 08/09/98. Nottingham Forest 0 Everton 2 (Ferguson 2).
The Blues' braveheart put his side in front when he nipped in front of young defender Craig Armstrong to power Michael Ball's left-wing cross past Dave Beasant. His second came seven minutes from time as he seized on a loose ball and fired a low left-foot shot into the far corner to seal the victory.

Goal 40. 03/10/98. Wimbledon 1 Everton 2 (Cadamarteri, Ferguson).
Fergie's fortieth sealed Everton's second win of the season as he leapt to head home David Unsworth's cross.

Goal 41. 28/10/98. League Cup. Middlesbrough 2 Everton 3 (Ferguson, Bakayoko, Hutchison).
Steve Vickers is made to pay for a mis-kicked clearance which puts Duncan in on goal - smashing his shot past an exposed Marlon Beresford.

Goal 42. 31/10/98. Everton 1 (Ferguson) Manchester United 4.

A consolation goal as Michael Ball's flighted free-kick is made by a trademark towering Ferguson header.

1998-99: Premiership: 13 apps, 4 goals. Cups 4 apps, 1 goals. Total: 17 apps, 5 goals.

Dunc's love for Everton is more than

SKIN DEEP

DO you know of any big name footballer who sports a tattoo on his arm designed by a fan of the club he loves? Duncan Ferguson did just that when he asked readers of The Evertonian magazine to send in their designs - and he chose his favourite one. Blood is thicker than water and it was a gesture that showed he was a fully fledged member of the special family that is Everton FC . . .

In the September 1997 edition of the Evertonian, Duncan declared that he wanted an Everton tattoo and asked readers of the magazine to design it.

Duncan intended to display his devotion to the club on the top of his left arm with the prize being that he would have the winning design applied in Indian ink.

As you might have expected, the sensational competition brought a tremendous response with hundreds of entries pouring in.

The designs ranged from the Scottish braveheart theme to Duncan's well-known love of pigeons.

In the end, Duncan opted for the famous number nine within the outline of the club crest and the motto: 'Nil Satis, Nisi Optimum.'

Duncan showed the design off when he posed for a front cover photograph for the January 1998 edition of the magazine.

The tattoo has adorned his upper left arm ever since - a permanent mark of his devotion to the Blues.

The big Scot broke his usual silence to thank readers of The Evertonian for their suggestions.

"I want to thank the supporters who took the time and trouble to send me ideas for the tattoo," he declared.

"They are what make Everton such a special club.

"They have supported me through good and bad times in the past and this is a small measure of my respect for them."

'I want to thank the supporters who took the time and trouble to send me ideas for the tattoo. They are what make Everton such a special club. They have supported me through good and bad'

THE BIG DU

Gavin Shelley, The Glen, Bebington, Wirral

Siobhan MacKenzie, Scarisbrick New Road, Southport

From pigeons to Braveheart - entries still flooding in!

There has been a tremendous response to our exclusive competition to design a tattoo for Duncan Ferguson.

Hundreds of entries have poured in and he will shortly be sifting through them before a winner is announced in next month's Evertonian.

The designs have ranged from the Scottish Braveheart theme through to Duncan's well-known love of pigeons.

Pictured are just a random selection of entries so far.

After he chooses the winning entry, Duncan will have the design emblazoned on the top of his arm.

Don't worry if you haven't sent in your design yet, because you still have until the end of the month in which to do so.

Entries should be sent to: Duncan Tattoo Competition, The Evertonian, PO Box 48, Old Hall Street, Liverpool L69 3EB.

Mark Weale, Welton Avenue, Wirral

Helen Cadman, Flint Court, Ellesmere Port

Jayne Clayton, Wadebridge Road, Stonebridge Park, Liverpool

Kate Daley, Dover Road, Maghull

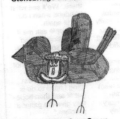

Andrew Makin, Scar Green Avenue, Norris Green

David Duke, Warbreck Moor, Liverpool

Vicky Winstanley, Firstone Grove, Kirkby

Rick Fazakerley, Southport Road, Ormskirk

NC TATTOO

Lisa Powell, Airdale Close, Birkenhead

BRAVE HEART

S. Brady (no address supplied)

Dean Struth, Mahon Avenue, Bootle

Ben Jonathan Williams, Sulby Avenue, Tuebrook

Paul Floyd Gladwell, Acrefield Court, Prenton (three entries)

DUNCAN FOREVER

Michael Lamb, Talbot Road, Great Sutton

A TRUE BLUE FLYER

Lisa Powell, Airdale Close, Birkenhead

GRIM REAPER

TRUE BLUE

Joanne Fletcher, Newick Road, Kirkby

Dion Patrick Jones, Sarn Lane, Hope, Nr Wrexham

Nikki Miller, Falcon Road, Ellesmere Port

David Wallbank, Garrowby Drive, Huyton

Nicola Batchen, Astley, Nr Manchester

Design for life: The pages from The Evertonian showing the designs sent in by fans for Duncan's tattoo

Ecstasy ... and agony

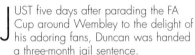

DUNCAN'S STORY: PART IV

JUST five days after parading the FA Cup around Wembley to the delight of his adoring fans, Duncan was handed a three-month jail sentence.

Found guilty of assault a fortnight earlier, he was sentenced to three months in jail at Glasgow Sheriff court but bailed just hours later after his lawyers made a successful application for appeal to the same sheriff.

Duncan was jailed despite social inquiry reports recommending a community service order. The appeal was put back to October. Everton's chairman Peter Johnson also presented a letter in support of the star praising his behaviour and highlighting his regular visits to children's hospitals.

Speaking afterwards, Duncan's lawyer, Donald Findlay QC, told the media: "I would imagine he is relieved. It now goes to the Appeal Court where the sheriff will have to give his grounds for conviction and sentence."

The decision freed Duncan to start the 1995-96 season as the additional 12-match ban could not be imposed until after the appeal had been heard.

Sentencing, Sheriff Alexander Eccles said: "This is not the first time you have been convicted of an incident of violence and I am taking into account your previous convictions.

"To bring home to you that this type of behaviour cannot be tolerated, and bearing in mind you are looked up to by young people, you will go to prison for three months."

Everton officials expressed their dismay at the verdict and even John McStay, the

Raith Rovers player he was found guilty of headbutting, said he did not want Duncan sent to jail.

The action had only been started when a video tape of the clash was sent to the Procurator Fiscal's office.

Dick Taylor, one of Duncan's earliest influences at Carse Thistle Boys Club, said: "He had a lot of provocation up here (Scotland). The situation was becoming very intense for the lad.

"He came in for abuse and was not prepared to take it. People were jealous of him.

"If anything he should get the same as Eric Cantona - and teach the kids football. That is what he is good at."

Meanwhile, Everton director Cliff Finch told the Liverpool Echo that the club had been inundated with letters of support from fans and well-wishers.

Duncan cleared his head during the summer, admitting to The Evertonian that he relished the opportunity to try and gain some relaxation.

"I did as little as possible, just resting really," he said. "I went to Scotland to see my mum and dad and I went to Daniel Amokachi's wedding in Tunisia. I went with a couple of mates for a few days and we had a great time."

But after playing in the opening two games of the new season, Duncan was struck down by a new groin injury. He underwent a second hernia operation which kept him out of action for two months.

The second week in October arrived and Duncan prepared for his fateful court appearance. >

Behind bars: A shocked Duncan Ferguson is led away to start his three month jail sentence

Before he headed north - he granted a fan an unusual request.

Carl Schofield, of Upton, near Chester, had a £55 tattoo of Duncan applied to his back and sought the star's signature underneath.

Duncan happily obliged, adding: "It's a good likeness. It does me justice."

A delighted Carl then rushed back to the tattooist to have the signature added in Indian ink before Duncan's signature started to fade.

On Wednesday, October 11th, Evertonians heard the news they could scarcely believe. Duncan Ferguson had been sent to jail.

Judges at Edinburgh Supreme Court threw out his appeal on the butting charge and he was led out of court handcuffed to a prison officer and taken by a police van to Glasgow's notoriously tough Barlinnie Prison to begin his three-month sentence.

Fans and club officials were stunned by the verdict after confidently believing the sentence would be reduced to a community service order.

Everton director Clifford Finch claimed the big striker had been the victim of a vendetta.

He said: "We don't feel that a jail sentence will do any good. He has had

an exemplary report from the social services people in Liverpool.

"I believe the Scottish courts are trying to make an example of Duncan. It seems like a vendetta against the lad."

Everton secretary Michael Dunford issued a formal statement saying: "We are bitterly disappointed that a young man carrying out his profession has been jailed for something for which we consider there would have been a more appropriate punishment."

Club chairman Peter Johnson had sent a letter to the court in which he explained that Duncan was a changed man since moving south.

Duncan's lawyer, John Mitchell QC, had argued before the three appeal judges that the sentence was excessive and Ferguson should be allowed to serve community service.

But Lord Justice Hope, the Lord Justice General and most senior judge in Scotland, gave the decision after he and the two other judges deliberated for just 10 minutes in what they described as "a tragic case."

He said: "We have reached a decision we could not be justified with interfering with the sentence.

"The sentence of three months in prison was effective and a deterrent and cannot

be described as excessive. We therefore refuse the appeal."

He added that the fact Ferguson was already on probation for another assault when the incident happened had to be taken very seriously.

Earlier, the court had heard letters in support of Ferguson.

Peter Johnson and manager Joe Royle heard the news of the appeal being quashed at the chairman's Park Foods headquarters in Birkenhead.

Johnson said: "We are bitterly disappointed. It is a most inappropriate sentence. To send a young man to jail who is in a job and is of no danger whatsoever to society is totally wrong.

"This incident didn't take place in the streets, but on a football pitch. It didn't even attract the attention of the referee or the linesmen at the time. There was no caution. I simply cannot understand why they have subsequently jailed Duncan.

"I have always found Duncan to be a pleasant, quiet lad.

"We are not condoning what he did or making excuses. But we have all seen football incidents which have been much more serious.

"We hoped that common sense would prevail today. I was with Joe Royle when the news came through that Duncan had been jailed. We were both totally shell-shocked."

Royle simply added that he was "amazed and stunned."

Team-mate David Unsworth gave the view from his team-mates, saying: "Everyone is upset. Duncan is a good mate and I was absolutely gutted when I heard. When you get to know him, he is a great lad who will do anything for anybody.

"We all believe Duncan is a victim of his reputation.

"We had talked before about the hard time he had from the media in Scotland, and he came down here with that reputation and proved what kind of a person he is by being as good as gold.

"People also conveniently ignore the massive amount of work he has done in his spare time for local charities and hospitals."

In the days following Duncan's sentencing, Blues fans put pen to paper to vent their feelings at what they saw as a huge injustice.

The letters pages of the Daily Post and the Liverpool Echo were full of anger. The Liverpool Echo summed up the local feeling in their leader column of October 12.

It said: 'One of Britain's most expensive footballers is today languishing in Scotland's grim Barlinnie Jail - at no small cost to the taxpayer and serving a sentence which it is difficult to see as serving any real purpose.

'Nobody will argue about the serious nature of the offence but the punishment meted out is open to question.'

Albert Tarleton, the friend asked to look after Duncan's pigeons while he was away, concurred.

Mr Tarleton, from the Burscough >

'I was absolutely gutted when I heard. He is a great lad who will do anything for anybody. We all believe Duncan is a victim of his reputation'

On the road to Wembley: Posing on a police motorbike with team-mate Neville Southall before the 1995 FA Cup final

'I am devastated and shall be visiting him in prison. Keeping pigeons is the perfect antidote to the pressures of football. Duncan's pigeons are all very tame and very good with him'

Homing Society, said: "I am devastated and shall be visiting him in prison. It is diabolical what has happened.

"Keeping pigeons is the perfect antidote to the pressures of football. Duncan's pigeons are all very tame and very good with him."

Many fans wrote personal letters of support to the striker. The club reported that they had been receiving batches of 100 letters a day and were sending them on as soon as they could.

Secretary Michael Dunford said: "The support has been tremendous as was expected. We are sending them up as quickly as they are coming in. We are also sending pictures done by children, which are lovely. We know they mean a lot to Duncan."

A spokesman for the Scottish Prison Service said that Ferguson had settled in well.

Meanwhile, a former Barlinnie inmate told the Liverpool Echo that Duncan's arrival caused 'a buzz' at the prison.

The man, a trusted inmate who was released soon after Duncan's arrival, revealed: "The arrival of Big Dunc caused a bit of a buzz. We were all sympathetic towards him.

"None of the inmates could believe he had been jailed for what he did. He has a cell on his own.

"I got all his gear together when he arrived and showed him to his cell. I sat with him for a while and gave him some solid advice about prison life.

"I told him always to remember that although he is a big boy there are always bigger men in prison."

After arriving, he was forced to swap his clothes for regulation uniform. Slopping out continued at the prison and Duncan was up and at work in the hospital wing of the jail by 8am each day.

On November 7th, Duncan broke his silence in an open letter to fans in the Liverpool Echo.

The following day, Ferguson and Everton received another blow when it was announced the 12-match ban imposed on him by the Scottish FA was upheld by an independent tribunal.

Manager Royle said: "The attitude all along has been that Duncan Ferguson will be made an example of.

"It would appear that both the Scottish FA and their English counterparts have turned their backs on the player.

Big news: Duncan attempts to make his way to court as a massive press scramble to get the big story unfolds

"Who would blame Duncan if he wanted nothing whatsoever to do with either of them again? Certainly not me."

By the end of the week, Everton had taken an unprecedented step for a football club - petitioning for a judicial review north of the border. The club had to take the action because all national channels available had to be exhausted before the European Court of Human Rights could be called in. Everton felt the tribunal decision had acted in 'double jeopardy' - causing an individual to have suffered twice for one crime.

While Duncan waited for the decision as to when he could start playing again, he left prison on the morning of Friday, November 24th and headed straight back to Merseyside.

A burgundy Daimler hired by the club collected him from inside the jail and flashed past 30 waiting journalists just after 6.30am. He acknowledged fans for their support at the following day's home game against Sheffield Wednesday and resumed training the following week.

Bizarrely, Duncan's 44 days in jail served as the inspiration for Finnish composer Osmo Tapio Raihala who produced a piece of work entitled *Barlinnie Nine*. Everton fan Raihala said of his work: "I got the idea for it when he was facing jail and had just become something of a cult figure for Everton. It takes into account the contradictions in him: he has an aggressive side but there is a lyrical undertone to him, as the fact that he keeps pigeons shows."

Barlinnie Nine was premiered on April 20, 2005 by the Finnish Radio Symphony Orchestra in the Finlandia Hall, Helsinki - the same day Ferguson scored the only goal in the Blues' 1-0 victory over Manchester United at Goodison Park.

'The attitude all along has been that Duncan Ferguson will be made an example of. Both the Scottish FA and their English counterparts have turned their backs on the player'

Duncan's message to the fans

'I have been keen to express my thoughts to the thousands of people on Merseyside - and elsewhere in the country - who have been urging me to keep my head up. I can assure you that I have been doing just that. I owe it to the Evertonians who are right behind me'

Support: Everton fans showed their loyalty towards Duncan Ferguson in many different ways

DEAR EVERTONIANS,

I have been overwhelmed by the fantastic support I have received from Everton fans everywhere.

I can tell you that it has helped to keep my spirits up throughout the most difficult period in my life. The amount of mail I have received - and continue to receive - is enormous. I spend a tremendous amount of time reading your letters.

Obviously I am limited on the number of replies I can send out at the moment. But my family have been collecting the letters and taking them away for safe-keeping. I'm going to reply personally to every supporter who has taken the time and trouble to write to me. Those messages have been coming in by the sackful and it is going to be a major job dealing with them. But the office girls at Goodison will help me and it is something I want to do.

I feel it is very important to tell people just how much those messages have helped to lift my spirits.

I would also like to thank the club for being so supportive. To be honest I really didn't realise just how much I would miss Everton and the fans. I have been made to feel very much at home on Merseyside since I moved down from Scotland. Many friends have been wanting to show their support in a personal way by coming to see me in Barlinnie.

But in truth, it's really not the kind of place that I want to see people. For the time being, I'm just happy to receive those letters which keep me in touch with Merseyside.

I was pleased to see my manager Joe Royle, club chairman Peter Johnson and director Clifford Finch last night.

They were able to pass on some messages from my team-mates as well as bring me up to date with everything that is happening at the club. In my own way, I have been trying to keep in touch. I've got a radio and I wait anxiously to hear our results.

I was actually able to tune into the recent Feyenoord game in Holland. The lads played well and I was disappointed for them - and our travelling supporters - that we didn't get the result we deserved. I would have given anything to have been out there helping the lads.

I didn't realise just how much I would miss football. Obviously, I have no special privileges up here. But I am trying to keep as fit as I possibly can under the circumstances. I am able to exercise for up to an hour a day and I put as much into it as is possible.

I have been keen to express my thoughts to the thousands of people on Merseyside - and elsewhere in the country - who have been urging me to keep my head up. I can assure you that I have been doing just that. I owe it to the Evertonians who are right behind me.

Through the Echo, can I once again thank you for your continued support. I can't wait to pull on the blue shirt again and repay everybody in the only way I know how...on the football field.

Duncan Ferguson

Flowering for Scotland - then making a stand

Duncan seemed to have all the qualities to make him fully equipped for the challenge of leading the line for Scotland.

As things panned out, he would win just seven caps before deciding to bring his international career to an end at the age of 25.

He made his senior Scotland debut under Andy Roxburgh at the Mile High Stadium in Denver on May 17th, 1992, replacing Pat Nevin five minutes into the second half of the Scots' 1-0 friendly victory in the USA.

He wore the number 20 shirt and made an impressive start.

Three days later he was handed his full debut in another friendly against Canada in Toronto, playing 55 minutes in a 3-1 win before being replaced by Brian McClair.

His displays were enough to earn him a place in the Scottish squad for the 1992 European Championships in Sweden, but he made just one appearance in the finals, as a late substitute for McClair in a 1-0 defeat >

by Holland in Gothenburg.

But it was in his fourth appearance for the Tartan Army that Duncan really started to flourish. His powerful performance in a friendly against Germany at Ibrox was not enough to help the Scots avoid a 1-0 defeat but is said to have first alerted German giants Bayern Munich to his talents.

Duncan's first four caps all came during his time at Dundee United under Andy Roxburgh.

His fifth appearance was as an Everton player and under the management of Craig Brown.

Just days after becoming Everton's record signing, he joined the national squad for their friendly in Greece, playing his second successive full 90 minutes in the 1-0 European Championship qualifying defeat in Athens.

It would be another 20 months before he would pull on the national jersey again and, by now, he was starting to wonder about his future in the light of his treatment by the SFA.

He played in the goalless World Cup qualifiers against Austria and Estonia in the 1996-97 season but by October 1997, his mind was made up. Enough was enough.

He announced his international retirement and despite several coaches trying to talk him into a comeback, Duncan was not for turning.

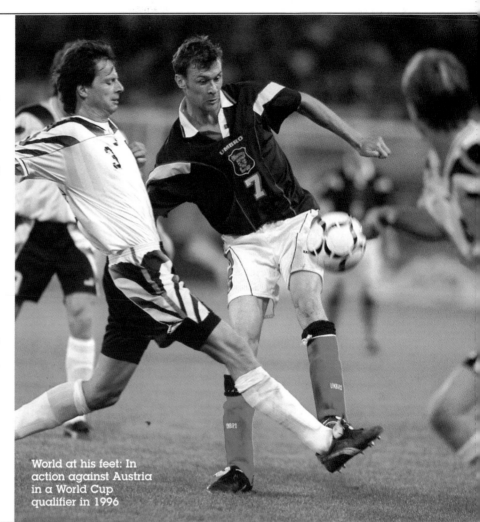

World at his feet: In action against Austria in a World Cup qualifier in 1996

Work and play: In Under-21 action in 1993 and (right) joking with Tommy Boyd

Relaxed: Training in Monaco in 1997

DUNCAN'S INTERNATIONAL RECORD

May 17th, 1992. Mile High Stadium, Denver. Friendly International. USA 0 Scotland 1 (Nevin 7). Attendance: 24,157.
Scotland: Marshall; McKimmie, McPherson (Whyte, 82), McLaren, Malpas; McCall, McAllister, McStay (McInally, 68), Nevin (Ferguson, 50); McCoist (Bowman, 77), McClair.

May 20th, 1992. Varsity Stadium, Toronto. Friendly International. Canada 1 Scotland 3 (McAllister 23, 87 (pen.), McCoist 68). Attendance: 10,872.
Scotland: Smith; Gough, McPherson, McLaren, Boyd; McCall (McKimmie 89), McAllister, McStay; Durie (Malpas 78), Ferguson (McClair 55), McCoist.

June 12th, 1992. Ullevi Stadium, Gothenburg. UEFA European Championships. Holland 1 Scotland 0. Attendance: 35,720.
Scotland: Goram; McKimmie, Gough, McPherson, Malpas; Durie, McCall, McStay, McAllister; McCoist (Gallacher 73), McClair (Ferguson 78).

March 24th, 1993. Ibrox. Friendly International. Scotland 0 Germany 1. Attendance: 36,400.
Scotland: Walker; Wright (Booth 64), Levein, McLaren, Irvine, Boyd; Bowman, Collins, McInally; Robertson, Ferguson.

December 18th, 1994. Olympic Stadium, Athens. UEFA European Championships. Greece 1 Scotland 0. Attendance: 7,976.
Scotland: Goram (Leighton 78); McKimmie (Spencer 46), Hendry, McLaren, Boyd; McKinlay, McCall, Collins, McAllister; McGinlay, Ferguson.

August 31st, 1996. Ernst Happel Stadium, Vienna. FIFA World Cup Qualifying. Austria 0 Scotland 0. Attendance: 29,500.
Scotland: Goram; Burley, Calderwood, Hendry, Boyd; McKinlay, McCall, Collins, McAllister; Ferguson, McCoist (Durie 75).

February 11th, 1997. Stade Louis II, Monaco. FIFA World Cup Qualifying. Estonia 0 Scotland 0. Attendance: 4,000.
Scotland: Goram; McNamara (McKinlay 75), Calderwood, Hendry, Boyd; Gallacher, McStay (I Ferguson 63), Collins, McAllister; Ferguson, McGinlay (McCoist 75).

THERE'S a fine line between showing the desire to win that strikes fears into defenders and the raw emotion that leaves referees reaching for their back pocket. Dunc has crossed that line on a few occasions but would we have him any other way? Perhaps there was no choice . . .

Passion player

From the moment he first pulled on the royal blue shirt, he has given his all for the cause and quickly established his reputation as an Everton icon.

At times his aggression and will to win saw him get on the wrong side of officials and he gained a reputation which led to him becoming the joint most sent-off player in Premiership history with eight dismissals, a dubious distinction he shares with Patrick Vieira.

No-one is suggesting he was a saint but there is no question that he also found himself on the wrong end of a few pieces of rough justice. His first dismissal in Everton colours came at Highbury in January 1995 when he pushed Arsenal's John Jensen in the chest and the Dane fell to the floor theatrically clutching his face.

Two months later, he was given his marching orders at Leicester following an aerial challenge with Jimmy Willis. To the amazement of everyone, including Willis, he was shown a red card by Paul Durkin. Willis even tried to help Duncan in his bid to have the card rescinded.

There's no excuses but take away Duncan's passion? He simply would not have been the same player . . .

DUNCAN'S DISMISSALS

1 v Arsenal (a) 14/01/95.
Referee: Robbie Hart.
Pushes John Jensen in the chest and the
Dane falls to the floor, clutching his face.

2 v Leicester (a) 04/03/95.
Referee: Paul Durkin. Dismissed for an
elbow on Jimmy Willis despite the Leicester
man later helping him fight his cause in
trying to overturn the red card.

3 v Blackburn (a) 21/09/96
Referee: David Elleray. Received two
bookings for foul and abusive language.

4 v Derby (h) 14/02/98.
Referee: Steve Dunn. Saw red after an
altercation with Paulo Wanchope.

5 v Bolton (h) 01/04/02.
Referee: Steve Bennett.
Given his marching orders following an
altercation with Fredi Bobic.

6 v Leicester (a) 20/03/03.
Referee: Barry Knight.
Booked first for catching Nikos Dabizas in
the face with his arm and a second time for
wrestling Steffen Freund to the ground.

7 v Charlton (a) 28/12/04.
Referee: Mike Riley. Banished for flailing an
elbow into Hermann Hreidarsson's face.

8 v Wigan (a) 31/01/06.
Referee: Mike Dean. Saw red for flooring
Wigan's Paul Scharner.

WELCOME HOME

DUNCAN

A happy homecoming . . .

DUNC'S STORY: PART V

. . . and a shock exit

On December 6th, 1995, an Edinburgh court put the final seven games of Duncan's SFA suspension on hold after Everton won a judicial review on account of him being punished twice for the same act.

The following night, Ferguson's first appearance in an Everton shirt for four months attracted 10,432 fans to a reserve team game against Newcastle.

Looking sharp, strong and full of running, he scored twice in a 5-0 win. >

Back in business: Bagpipe players heralded Duncan's first return to action after his spell in jail – in a reserve game! Fergie scored two goals in a 5-0 thrashing of Newcastle Reserves watched by a crowd of more than 10,000

Soon afterwards, he made his first team comeback as a substitute as Everton recorded their biggest win of the season to that point - a 3-0 defeat of West Ham - in front of the television cameras. Just hours later he was back in action in a practice match against Chester as the Blues looked to step up his return to match fitness.

He scored his first goals of the season with a brace in the New Year's Day win at Wimbledon. Surprisingly, they were also Duncan's first goals for Everton away from Goodison Park.

February arrived with good news for Duncan and the Blues with Judge Lord McFadyen quashing the final seven

games of his FA suspension after ruling the Scottish governing body had acted beyond their powers.

His treatment from the SFA had left him pondering his international future but the decision to miss Euro '96 was forced upon him when Everton withdrew him from the international squad on account of persistent groin trouble.

The 1996/97 season began in style for Duncan with the big striker upstaging £15 million capture Alan Shearer on his debut for Newcastle by leading Everton to a 2-0 victory. Three days later he scored twice at Old Trafford as Everton held champions Manchester United to a 2-2 draw.

In September, he was sent off by David Elleray at Blackburn for using "industrial language", not aimed at the referee but still enough to offend the public school master.

He was then troubled by further injury niggles but returned as a substitute in a 1-1 draw at Anfield and embarked on his longest unbroken league run for the club - 26 games until the end of the season.

By May he had netted 10 league goals to finish as the club's leading scorer as the Blues escaped relegation, including vital equalisers against West Ham and Liverpool.

In October 1997, Leeds manager George Graham shocked Everton officials

Upstaging Alan Shearer on his Newcastle debut, getting married ... and shock news as anxious fans wait at Bellefield

by claiming the club was trying to offload the big striker to Elland Road.

Graham said: "Everton are drumming up publicity by trying to link us with this player."

The club denied these suggestions but a little more than a year later, fans' favourite Fergie was on his way out of Goodison.

Just days before the Leeds link, it was the Scottish national team that had provided the Duncan-related headlines.

After careful consideration, the striker had announced his international retirement at the age of 25 after winning seven caps.

Talking about his player's decision, Howard Kendall said: "I've had a chat with Duncan and the Scotland manager Craig Brown on the matter.

"When Duncan brought up the issue, we discussed it at great length. Those conversations will remain private."

His decision did not go down well north of the border but few Evertonians were disappointed by his decision.

Now able to concentrate solely on his club career, Duncan scored the first hat-trick of his Everton career in December 1997 as the Blues recorded a vital 3-2 victory over relegation rivals Bolton Wanderers. His treble kicked off the best goalscoring form of his Goodison career - seven goals in eight matches as the Blues hauled themselves clear of the bottom three.

In February 1998, Duncan was officially made club captain by Howard Kendall after Gary Speed's refusal to travel to West Ham and subsequent transfer to Newcastle. A number of inspirational performances, plus another goal against Liverpool, maintained a depleted Everton side's battle for survival.

Heartbreak: For one sad Dunc fan

As the season came to a close, Duncan was becoming increasingly troubled by a knee injury. But again he underlined his commitment to the cause by finishing as the club's leading scorer, this time with 11 goals.

A personal highlight came in June 1998 when he married girlfriend Janine Tasker at Liverpool's Anglican Cathedral.

Duncan's first goals as a newly-wed came with a brace at Nottingham Forest in September which gave Everton a 2-0 win. His 40th goal in Everton colours gave the Blues their second away win the following month as his header helped to serve up victory at Wimbledon.

But after netting in the 3-2 League Cup triumph at Middlesbrough and grabbing a consolation goal in a 4-1 defeat at home to Manchester United, >

'The club denied these suggestions but a little more than a year later, fans' favourite Fergie was on his way out of Goodison'

'As the silence from the boardroom spoke volumes, Smith indicated that he was ready to resign from his position as manager. Finally, a joint statement between chairman and manager was issued ...'

Duncan was on his way out of Goodison, joining Newcastle for a fee of £7m.

The saga unravelled - literally - during the Blues' Premiership match against the Magpies on November 23rd, 1998.

Manager Walter Smith insisted he had no knowledge of the sale.

As the silence from the boardroom spoke volumes, Smith indicated that he was ready to resign from his position as manager.

Finally, almost a week after Ferguson headed to Tyneside, a joint statement between chairman and manager was issued.

It read: 'After four months in the manager's seat, having spent £20 million on six new players, bringing the squad total to 35, Walter Smith assessed his playing staff and discussed with the chairman his plans for the future.

'Having seen the manager's report, the chairman emphasised to him the requirement to sell players to return the squad to reasonable proportions.

'The club had received a substantial offer for Duncan Ferguson earlier in the season, which was rejected.

'The chairman and manager agreed that any future offer should be given serious consideration.

'The club then became aware of Newcastle's interest.

'Events started moving rapidly last Monday evening.

'A substantial offer for Duncan Ferguson was received from Newcastle United, which was discussed with that club's representatives immediately before, and during, the course of last Monday evening's game.

'Their discussions resulted in an agreement being reached at that time. Unfortunately, details of these discussions were not passed to Walter Smith during the course of the game, and it is regretted that he learned of the final agreement reached regarding Duncan Ferguson, in the manner he did, subsequent to the conclusion of the match.'

Irrespective of the ins and outs of the transfer and the question marks raised over the running of the club, the bottom line was that Everton fans had lost a hero.

Dun and dusted: Duncan models the Newcastle kit with new strike partner Alan Shearer and manager Ruud Gullit – leaving behind unhappy Everton fans

'I will never, ever forget the Everton fans ...
When I was in jail, it was a difficult time and they stuck by me ...
Everton fans will be part of my blood ...
Getting to captain and wearing the number nine shirt meant so much ...
I wish I could have had more success and scored more goals ...
I wish the fans I am leaving behind all the best and I
hope Everton can get up to where they belong ...'

'I may have left but I will never, ever forget the Everton fans and I mean that. They will be with me forever. When I was in jail it was a very difficult time in my career and my life and the fans stuck by me. All the letters I got then I appreciated so much; they made a hell of a difference. Everything they were saying to me, I will remember. They were encouraging me and saying keep your chin up. It did help.

The support I received from the people of Liverpool was special. Everton fans will be part of my blood because of the way they stood by me. Their loyalty to me was one of the main reasons why I love Everton so much.

I will always have fond memories of the club. Getting to captain the club and wearing the number nine shirt after so many other great names meant a lot to me. Maybe you don't realise how much at the time, but I did genuinely love the fans and the club. Hopefully they will see me as someone who put his heart into the club and did his best for them. I like Liverpool. I like the city, the way of life, the Scousers. I must do, I married one.

But I would like to think my Everton career has been successful. Everton bought me for £4m, have sold me for £8m, and they have had four years' service out of me.

I would say the highlight was definitely the FA Cup win, but I am proud of never having been on the losing side in a derby. It was

frustrating that I never had a settled partner during my time at the club and that we never really played with a winger. I wish I could have had more success and scored more goals for the fans, but that isn't just down to Duncan Ferguson. It is down to the whole team and one player cannot make all the difference.

For four or five years, I'd say creating chances has been a problem. Hopefully, Bakayoko can be the answer. You have to give him time to settle in, but we'll never know if it would have worked alongside me because I am not there anymore.

I was settled in Liverpool and now I am going to have to get settled in Newcastle. But that is the life of a footballer I suppose, I know that.

It is difficult, but you have to fit in. I have joined another massive club. Newcastle represents my future and I have to do my best for them.

But I wish the fans I am leaving behind all the best and I hope Everton can get up to where they belong because the supporters deserve that,

They need to be successful.
I will miss them and send them my love'

Duncan Ferguson
(A personal message to fans printed in The Evertonian magazine after his departure to Newcastle in 1998)

'I didn't want to sell him.

ALTER SMITH sold Duncan twice – although he didn't want to on either occasion.

In August 1997, Walter spoke to The Evertonian about his regret at letting Duncan go when he was manager of Rangers.

Smith would get to know Everton well in the years ahead but at the time was in town to manage the 'team of nations' in Dave Watson's testimonial.

He said: "I didn't really want to sell him and no-one at the club wanted to. We would take him back but the difficulty is that he would find it very difficult to come back to Scotland. Rangers have such a high profile in Scotland and the same reasons why we had to sell him would still apply.

"We were sorry we came to the decision to let him go because that had nothing whatsoever to do with the football side of things.

"I rate him very highly as a player, but he was unfortunate at Rangers in as much as he came to the club maybe a year too early for his good.

"But as a player you are restricted if

– *Walter Smith*

one club wishes to sell you and another wishes to buy.

"We had Mark Hateley and Ally McCoist who had formed a terrific partnership over the previous season or so. So it was always going to be difficult for any player to come in and force his way into the reckoning straight away.

"Ironically as happens in these situations, as soon as he left for Everton, Ally McCoist broke his leg which would have given Duncan far more opportunity."

In 1998, Walter was in the Goodison hotseat when the deal to take Duncan to Newcastle United was agreed by then chairman Peter Johnson.

On November 24th, Smith told the Liverpool Echo: "During the course of the last week I was made aware by a number of people that attempts were being made by a number of people at the club to attract offers for Duncan Ferguson. I ignored this because the chairman had indicated to me that a number of clubs

were interested in him. However, as far as I was concerned, that interest did not constitute any kind of transfer move because Duncan Ferguson had been attracting that kind of transfer story for most of the season and was still an Everton player.

"On the Monday morning I received the same information, and with the rumours, I felt that it was necessary for me to talk, as manager, to Duncan. I spoke to him and told him I felt moves were afoot to try and sell him and that I would speak to the chairman before the game, as I usually do, to try and clarify the situation. That meeting never took place and, unknown to me, Duncan was transferred to Newcastle during that match.

"In football we are surrounded by speculation all the time and we have to live with it.

"At no time on Monday, and I stress at no time, was I made aware that Newcastle United had made an official bid, and even more to the point, that the club had accepted it and that Duncan Ferguson was in talks with a view to a transfer deal."

No-one at the club did ...'

Rebellion: Graffiti is daubed on the walls of Goodison Park sparked by the club's controversial decision to sell Duncan Ferguson – without the knowledge of manager Walter Smith

'At no time was I made aware Newcastle United had made an official bid, and even more to the point, that the club had accepted it and that Duncan Ferguson was in talks with a view to a transfer deal'

Duncan Ferguson

Back where

T HURSDAY, August 18th 2000 was to prove a Blue-letter day for Evertonians.

Blues owner Bill Kenwright had started speaking to Ferguson the previous tea-time and at 11.20pm that night, Ferguson jumped in his car, fastened the seatbelt and headed for Goodison.

Mr Kenwright said: "I was speaking to him to try to find a way through things and I said if you want to prove yourself to anyone, you should come and prove it in an Everton shirt. We started speaking on the phone at 5.30pm and by 9pm we were laughing; I knew we'd made a breakthrough. At 11.20pm he rang me to say he was in his car and on his way back home, and the word 'money' wasn't mentioned once."

The reception that greeted Ferguson outside Goodison confirmed that his reputation had not diminished in the slightest among Evertonians and after a day of stringent medical tests, he put pen

he belongs

to paper on a five-year contract with the Blues paying Newcastle £3.75m.

"To tell you the truth, if it wasn't Everton, I probably wouldn't have left Newcastle," he admitted. "It was Everton who were the club for me and that was the reason I moved.

"It's amazing when you play for Everton, it's an incredible feeling. It's in your blood and it's been in mine for the last four, five, six years; I just couldn't shake it. I settled in the area and was

comfortable in the city. My family is from here, I kept my house here and I'm just delighted to be back. I still have my tattoo, yes, and once Newcastle had decided they no longer required my services, there was never a doubt in my mind I would never knock back Everton."

He immediately took up where he had left off, scoring twice on his home 'debut' against Charlton but a nasty calf injury sustained in the same game left him sidelined for three months.

After only three games back in the side in January, he was ruled out again, this time after breaking his hand while defending himself during a break-in at his Rufford home.

Ferguson was the victim of an attempted burglary by two men at his former house in Rufford. He confronted the pair and was able to detain one of them. The second man managed to flee but was eventually caught. Both men were sentenced to 15 months' imprisonment. ❯

Fit again for the start of the 2001/02 season, Duncan scores penalties in each of the first two games of the season but then returns to the treatment table after sustaining an ankle injury.

A disappointing league campaign coupled with an extremely disappointing FA Cup quarter-final defeat at Middlesbrough saw Walter Smith's spell as manager come to an end.

Preston manager David Moyes replaced him and he named Duncan as captain for his first game in charge. The big man responded with an inspirational performance and went on to score four goals in six games before suspension brought a premature end to his season.

The 2002/03 campaign was something of a write-off as a back injury restricted Duncan to just six substitute appearances towards the end of the season.

The following season started little better and during November he was banned from Bellefield following a disagreement with Moyes but he eventually apologised and the matter was forgotten.

In early 2003, Duncan again fell victim to a case of burglary. This time there was only one intruder at his Formby home and, again, he confronted him. He restrained the man until police arrived.

Back on the pitch, he saw red at Leicester in March following an angry incident involving Steffen Freund which was followed by gestures to the home crowd.

He returned to the fold in time to end the season with a goal against Bolton.

The 2004-05 season would prove a fine one for Duncan and the Blues.

The big striker, in the final year of his Goodison contract, proved an incredibly influential figure both coming off the bench as a substitute and, occasionally, in a starting role.

His goals were worth a number of points as Everton recorded their best-ever Premiership finish of fourth and booked their place in the final qualifying round of the UEFA Champions League.

Duncan scored his first goal of the season from the penalty spot in September as Everton came through a tricky Carling Cup tie at Bristol City.

The following month he came on as a substitute to grab the winning goal in a thrilling 3-2 win over Norwich City at Carrow Road which cemented the Blues' place among the early Premiership pacesetters.

He provided another winner - this time in a tight affair at Goodison against Fulham - and in December supplied a timely equaliser on the stroke of half-time against Bolton as Everton came from behind to register an important 3-2 victory.

A week later he revelled in a brief appearance from the substitutes' bench as the Blues secured a sweet 1-0 derby success over Liverpool at Goodison - but the year ended badly for the big man. ❯

COUNT ME IN

Fergie agrees a contract as clubs finalise the fee

■DAVID PRENTICE reports from Goodison Park

DUNCAN FERGUSON signalled his intentions to make his ... Everton permanent by agreeing personal terms ...

'We started speaking on the phone at 5.30pm and by 9pm we were laughing; I knew we'd made a breakthrough. At 11.20pm he rang me to say he was in his car and on his way back home, and the word 'money' wasn't mentioned once'

Big news: The Echo reports on Fergie's triumphant retrun to Goodison — although not every fan was happy (see picture above)! Left: Reunited with Walter Smith

'It's amazing when you play for Everton, It's an incredible feeling. It's in your blood and it's been in mine for the last four, five, six years; I just couldn't shake it. I settled in the area and was comfortable in the city. My family is from here, I kept my house here and I'm just delighted to be back. I still have my tattoo, yes, and once Newcastle had decided they no longer required my services, there was never a doubt in my mind I would never knock back Everton'

Bombshell
Fergie OUT for season in injury shocker

EXCLUSIVE by VIC GIBSON

STAR STRIKER Duncan Ferguson faces a hernia operation that will rule him out for the rest of the season — including the FA Cup final against Manchester United on May 20.

That hammer blow for the Blues was delivered after Ferguson hobbled off just 30 minutes into Everton's 0-0 draw with Sheffield Wednesday at Hillsborough. The big Scot, playing his first game for almost five weeks because of suspension, suffered a recurrence of the groin strain which forced him to withdraw from Scotland's squad last month. Everton manager Joe Royle.

Speaking Exclusively to the *Daily Post* last night, revealed the full extent of the injury.

He said: "Duncan Ferguson patiently wasn't fit. We will be sending him to a specialist.

"We are deeply suspicious that he may have a hernia. If so, he will need an operation."

When pressed on the possible length of lay-off, Ferguson boss Royle added: "He is probably out of the cup final. That is something we have got to accept.

"But it is more important to get the injury done as soon as possible. We want it to heal.

Loss

"It has been nagging him a while. It just came on. It can't be put down to one man."

Eventful: Dunc's second spell at the club featured everything from great goals to injuries and red cards; a Champions League qualifier and a fairytale strike to round it all off

He was dismissed at The Valley just minutes after coming on as a late substitute at Charlton and forced to serve another suspension.

But he was back in the good books with a vengeance come April. Rolling back the years, he produced a vintage display against Manchester United, capping it all off by heading the only goal of the game in front of the Gwladys Street. He followed that up by scoring a late leveller in the home game against Birmingham to edge the Blues ever nearer the promised land of the Champions League.

His performances were enough to persuade David Moyes to offer him a new one-year deal in June, albeit on reduced terms. Duncan accepted and was even awarded the famous number nine shirt again. The Blues' last European campaign dated back to Duncan's time in Barlinnie so it was with extra relish that he prepared for the Champions League eliminators with Villarreal.

Everton pushed the skilful Spanish side all the way but after losing 2-1 at Goodison, he had a crucial 'goal' chalked off in the return leg in Spain to the bewilderment of almost everyone in the ground other than Italian referee Pierluigi Collina.

With injuries again making Duncan's season a stop-start affair, manager Moyes revealed in December that the big striker would consider his future early in the new year. He explained that Duncan had admitted to him that he was taking longer

to recover from matches and had expressed disappointment that he wasn't able to exert the same influence as in previous seasons.

After the win at Portsmouth in January, newspaper speculation hinted at a possible switch to Pompey but the suggestions were angrily dismissed by Moyes.

On the final day of the month, Duncan's topsy-turvy Blues career took another twist when he was sent off at Wigan within minutes of coming on as a substitute. It earned him the dubious distinction of joining Patrick Vieira as the most sent-off player in Premiership history with seven dismissals apiece.

The club penalty for his red card took the total paid out by the Blues man in fines to in excess of £200,000. He received a seven-game ban after the FA review footage of the incident - a decision which infuriated Moyes.

He returned to make half-a-dozen substitute appearances before being handed his first Premiership start since November 6th along with the captain's armband for an emotional farewell against West Brom on the final day of the season.

After being afforded a fine reception before kick off, Duncan saw his side fall 2-0 behind early in the second half but appeared to have given them hope when he headed home a Mikel Arteta cross - only for the goal to be chalked off for offside.

But when teenager Victor Anichebe scored his first senior goal late on, it

sparked a fightback from the Blues.

The game was in injury time when Mikel Arteta was tripped in the box and referee Alan Wiley pointed to the spot to tee up a fairytale finish for Duncan.

With regular penalty taker James Beattie sat in the stands due to injury, Arteta went to place the ball on the spot before being informed by James McFadden that it was likely to be the big man's final game.

Arteta revealed: "We got the penalty and Faddy came running over. He said: 'Mikky, Mikky, what are you doing? It's his last game!' I just said: 'Fine. Here, have it!' That's the way it was. I understand that he wanted to score."

In a heart-stopping moment, Ferguson's left-footed strike was saved by West Brom goalkeeper Tomasz Kuszczak but the rebound came straight back to the big Scot and he scored from the rebound via the Polish keeper's knee.

Goodison roared. It seemed fitting that the Everton icon's final act in a Blue shirt should be to score at the Gwladys Street End.

As the players returned for the customary end-of-season lap of honour, all eyes turned to Ferguson, whose four children had been mascots for the day. He applauded the faithful, mouthing: 'Every one of you is quality,' unable to hold back the odd tear as he took the applause of the Evertonians.

The flag thrown to him said it all: 'Once A Blue, Always A Blue...thanks for the memories.'

HERE'S the second part of our goals rundown, featuring Dunc's strikes in a blue shirt from number 43 to his farewell effort against West Brom at Goodison Park . . .

2000-01.

Goals 43 and 44.
23/08/2000. Everton 3 (Jeffers, Ferguson 2) Charlton 0.
Ferguson marked his return from Newcastle with a timely late double. First he surged on to a Thomas Gravesen pass to drill home the second goal with six minutes left. Second, in injury-time, he drove home another via a slight deflection from Richard Rufus.

Goal 45. 07/02/01.
Everton 2 (Ferguson, Campbell) Leeds United 2.
Nigel Martyn conceded four times to Big Dunc. On this occasion, a rare misjudgement from Nigel saw Thomas Gravesen's lob break to the edge of the area where Duncan prodded it calmly back into the net.

Goal 46. 08/04/01.
Everton 3 (Ferguson, Ball, Weir) Manchester City 1.
Duncan swept home the equaliser after Kevin Campbell's touch presented him with a shooting opportunity.

Goal 47. 16/04/01.
Everton 2 (Ferguson, Unsworth) Liverpool 3.
Kevin Campbell won a high ball lofted into the box by Michael Ball and, although Jamie Carragher got in a block, the ball spun invitingly into the path of Ferguson who drilled home an equaliser.

Goal 48. 28/04/ 2001.
Everton 2 (Ferguson, Alexandersson) Bradford City 1.
Michael Ball's long throw from the left was flicked on by Kevin Cambell for Ferguson to turn and fire home from inside the six-yard box.

2000-01:
Premiership: 9+3 apps, 6 goals.
Cups: 1 apps, 0 goals.
Total: 10+3 apps, 6 goals.

Deadly DUNC Part II

43

2001-02.

Goal 49. 18/08/01.
Charlton 1 Everton 2 (Ferguson (pen.), Weir).
Duncan is on penalty duty and sends Dean Kiely the wrong way from the spot after Chris Powell had tripped Kevin Campbell.

Goal 50. 20/08/01.
Everton 1 (Ferguson (pen.)) Tottenham Hotspur 1.
Another penalty after David Elleray deemed Gary Doherty to have brought down Kevin Campbell in the box.

Goal 51. 12/09/01.
League Cup. Everton 1 (Ferguson (pen.)) Crystal Palace 1.
Duncan is spot on again after defender Tony Popovic held back Kevin Campbell and referee John Brandwood awarded a penalty.

Goal 52. 26/01/02.
FA Cup. Everton 4 (OG, Ferguson, Campbell 2) Leyton Orient 1.
Paul Gascoigne - enjoying one of his best games in an Everton shirt - shrugged off two defenders before teeing up Ferguson who side-footed home from 10 yards.

Goal 53. 16/03/02.
Everton 2 (Unsworth, Ferguson) Fulham 1.
Duncan marks David Moyes's first game in charge by chasing down a clearance from Fulham keeper Edwin van der Sar and slotting home Everton's second goal in the 13th minute as the new regime got off to a winning start.

Goal 54. 23/03/02.
Derby County 3 Everton 4 (Unsworth, Stubbs, Alexandersson, Ferguson).
Duncan picked his spot from two-yards out to make it 4-1 with 19 minutes remaining, firing past Derby's Swiss keeper Patrick Foletti on his only full start for the Rams.

Goal 55. 29/03/02.
Newcastle United 6 Everton 2 (Ferguson, Alexandersson).
David Unsworth's throw bounced off Andy O'Brien and Ferguson scooped a shot goalwards. Despite his best efforts, Toon keeper Shay Given could not keep it out.

Goal 56. 13/04/02.
Everton 2 (Chadwick, Ferguson) Leicester City 2.
Duncan nets the Everton equaliser four minutes from time with his 50th league goal for the club.
  David Unsworth's curling free-kick from the left flank fell to Ferguson, who stabbed it home from close range.

2001-02:
Premiership: 17+5 apps, 6 goals.
Cups: 3 apps, 2 goals.
Total: 20+5 apps, 8 goals.

2002-03:
Premiership: 0+7 apps, 0 goals.
Cups: 0+1 apps, 0 goals.
Total: 0+8 apps, 0 goals.

2003-04.

Goal 57. 13/09/03.
Everton 2 (Radzinski, Ferguson (pen.)) Newcastle United 2.
Another late leveller, this time from the penalty spot. Jermain Jenas brought down Tomasz Radzinski and Ferguson stepped up to smash the ball home and earn Everton a share of the spoils.

Goals 58 and 59.
24/09/03. **League Cup.**
Everton 3 (Ferguson 2 (1 pen.), Chadwick) Stockport County 0.
After opening the scoring from the penalty spot, Duncan completed a double with Everton's third after a fine run from James McFadden.

Goal 60. 28/09/03.
Everton 4 (Watson 3, Ferguson)
Leeds United 0.
Tony Hibbert's right-wing cross is met by an unmarked Ferguson who headed home from six-yards.

Goal 61. 26/12/03.
Manchester United 3
Everton 2 (OG, Ferguson).
A late goal as Duncan stooped to head home at the back post after Gary Naysmith's cross eluded Francis Jeffers.

Goals 62 and 63.
03/01/04. **FA Cup. Everton 3 (Kilbane, Ferguson 2 (2 pens)) Norwich City 1.**
Twice stepped up to roll home spot-kicks after two fouls by Iwan Roberts on Alan Stubbs.

60

57

Goal 64. 21/02/04.
Southampton 3 Everton 3
(Rooney 2, Ferguson).
Duncan nets with a deft header from a
Thomas Gravesen cross from the left to
put the Blues two goals to the good at St
Mary's.

Goal 65. 08/05/04.
Everton 1 (Ferguson)
Bolton Wanderers 2.
A fine goal with Duncan sweeping home
from six-yards after neat approach play
by Wayne Rooney, Tomasz Radzinski
and Leon Osman.

2003-04:
Premiership: 13+7 apps, 5 goals.
Cups: 4 apps, 4 goals.
Total: 17+7 apps, 9 goals.

2004-05

Goal 66. 22/09/04.
League Cup. Bristol City 2
Everton 2 (Ferguson (pen.),
Chadwick).
Duncan scored from the spot after Kent
referee Phil Crossley awarded the Blues
a 29th-minute penalty.

Goal 67. 23/10/04.
Norwich City 2 Everton 3
(Kilbane, Bent, Ferguson).
After surrendering a two-goal lead,
supersub Duncan grabbed the winner
with a superb far post header from Steve
Watson's deep cross.

Goal 68. 20/11/04.
Everton 1 (Ferguson) Fulham 0.
Ferguson again comes up with the all-
important goal after coming off the
bench. Thomas Gravesen curled the ball
into the box and although Kevin Kilbane
saw a fine header pushed out by keeper
Mark Crossley, the Blues' talisman
ducked to nod the loose ball into the
bottom corner.

Goal 69. 04/12/04. Everton 3
(Ferguson, Gravesen, OG)
Bolton Wanderers 2.
Duncan drew Everton level in first half
injury-time when he met an Alessandro
Pistone cross and Jussi Jaaskelainen could
only turn his effort into the net off a post.

Goal 70. 20/04/05.
Everton 1 (Ferguson)
Manchester United 0.
Duncan rolls back the years when he
wriggles free of Rio Ferdinand to head
home Mikel Arteta's 55th minute free-kick
and seal a vital three points in the Blues'
bid for Europe.

67

Goal 71. 23/04/05.
Everton 1 (Ferguson)
Birmingham City 1.
A late equaliser, spinning to score at the far post after Maik Taylor had saved at Tim Cahill's feet.

2004-05:
Premiership: 6+29 apps, 5 goals.
Cups: 2 apps, 1 goal.
Total: 8+29 apps, 6 goals.

Goal 72. 07/05/06.
Everton 2 (Anichebe, Ferguson)
West Brom 2.
Scored with his final touch in an Everton shirt, drilling home the rebound after having his initial penalty saved.

2005-06:
Premiership: 7+20 apps, 1 goal.
Cups: 3+3 apps, 0 goals.
Total: 10+23 apps, 1 goal.

TOTAL GOALS: Headers: 39
Shots: 25 **Penalties:** 8.

Who Let The Goals In?

Nigel Martyn	4
Peter Schmeichel	4
David James	3
Kevin Pressman	3
Mark Crossley	3
Gavin Ward	3
Dean Kiely	3
Robert Green	3
Shay Given	2
Nick Colgan	2
Tim Howard	2
Jussi Jaaskelainen	2
Hans Segers	2
Steve Ogrizovic	2
Maik Taylor	2
Kevin Miller	2
Dave Beasant	2
Gary Walsh	2
Neil Sullivan	2
John Lukic	1
Craig Forrest	1
Simon Tracey	1
Neil Edwards	1
Paul Musselwhite	1
Lionel Perez	1
Fraser Digby	1
David Seaman	1
Ludek Miklosko	1
Tim Flowers	1
Ed de Goey	1
David Watson	1
Neil Sullivan	1
Marlon Beresford	1
Nicky Weaver	1
Sander Westerveld	1
Matt Clarke	1
Scott Barrett	1
Edwin van der Sar	1
Patrick Foletti	1
Ian Walker	1
Paul Robinson	1
Antti Niemi	1
Steve Phillips	1
Tomasz Kuszczak	1

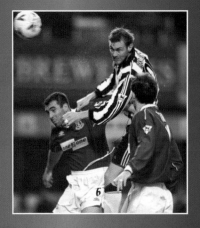

ONE of Duncan's big interviews came after he returned for his second spell at Everton in 2000. He spoke honestly about his hopes for the future – and his desire to rid himself of his injury jinx . . .

'When I have been injured sometimes you feel as if people think you want to be injured. I am desperate to play football and stay injury-free'

THEY say you should never go back - but Evertonians the world over were delighted when Duncan returned to his spiritual home in August 2000.

But the man himself was even more delighted.

In a rare interview, he explained his feelings in an exclusive chat with The Evertonian.

"It seems like I've never been away to tell you the truth. There are a lot of different faces here but I know all the backroom staff, all the security fellas and the cooks and all that and they are all the same. It feels like I have just come back home.

"Because I had such an affection for the club you are always thinking in the back of your mind that maybe one day you will be back but you don't know with football."

What had begun back in October 1994 as a three month loan spell turned into the stuff dreams are made of as with every leap, header and flick-on, Ferguson wrote himself into Goodison folklore.

Yet a string of injuries often interrupted what had always threatened to be a truly glorious career. After a successful start to his second spell, Ferguson once again found himself back in the treatment room.

But if the fans find the Scot's frequent   >

DUNCAN EXCLUSIVE

lay-offs frustrating, they want to be in the boots of the man himself.

"To tell you the truth when I have been injured sometimes you feel as if people think you want to be injured. But I am maybe trying harder than anything to get myself fit to play for this club.

"I am desperate to play football and stay injury-free.

"Obviously you are going to get criticised but it is strange really to get criticised just because you are injured - as if you want to be injured.

"It seems to be a wee jinx with me at the moment. I think when I left Everton and went to Newcastle, the injuries started. But last year I played more than 20 games so it wasn't as bad as everyone made out.

"You are always going to get criticised but the only criticism I am interested in is my manager's. So at the end of the day as far as I am concerned, I have just got to prove my fitness.

"When I have played, I have thought I have done well but when I have been injured it has been very difficult.

"I think when I am fit I can do a job, you know. I think when I had a wee run last year at Newcastle if you spoke to the likes of Alan Shearer and anyone who played alongside me, they would say that when I got myself fit I did a decent job.

"The thing is that you want to play consistently and maybe play 20 games on the spin and then you can start to get a bit of form. It is very difficult to come back and play four or five games, be out for a month and then come back and play another three or four.

"Because, as every professional footballer will tell you, it takes you a couple of months to get back properly. So, that has been the hardest, to stop and start."

As you would expect, the big centre-forward admits that he strives for quality service from the flanks.

"I have said it before, every striker at every club screams for service. When I was at Newcastle, Alan Shearer and myself were screaming for wingers and it seems to be the same thing everywhere.

"Centre forwards need crosses,

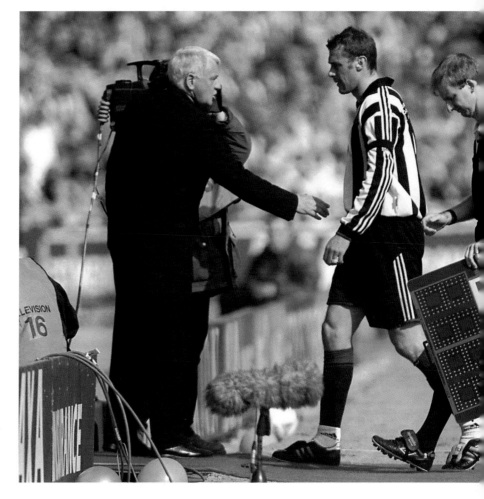

especially myself. Obviously I would benefit from a lot more crosses from the wing, I think most strikers would do anyway.

"I think it would be nice to score a lot of goals while I am here, I think everybody wants to score more goals but there is more to my game than that.

"There will always be some people in the game that are just goalscorers but I think I can contribute quite a lot to the team even if I don't score. But as far as targets go I am just trying to play as many games as I possibly can."

Fergie has always enjoyed a fantastic relationship with the supporters and was welcomed back with the warmth you

would expect for a returning hero.

"I've had a good rapport with the fans and they can obviously see that I am a tryer and I want to be here, I've proved that, I can't prove my loyalty more than I have already done.

"I just want to work hard and play well and show them that myself and the team are going to go out and do their best for them.

"I said I'd like to end my career here last time I was here. I was more than happy at Everton then.

"I would have signed for life at the time. Obviously I've signed a five-year contract now and I think that speaks for itself."

'I have said it before, every striker at every club screams for service. When I was at Newcastle, Alan Shearer and myself were screaming for wingers and it seems to be the same thing everywhere. Centre forwards need crosses, especially myself'

'I've had a good rapport with the fans and they can obviously see that I am a tryer and I want to be here, I've proved that, I can't prove my loyalty more than I have already. I said I'd like to end my career here'

Derby
DEST

WHEN he saw red, you knew
Duncan was in the mood . . .

ROYER

From the moment he headed Andy Hinchcliffe's corner past David James for his first Everton goal in November 1994, Duncan struck fear into the Reds.

He relished nothing more than a derby duel and always seemed to save his best for games against Liverpool and fellow North-West rivals Manchester United.

But it was in the clashes with Liverpool where he really shone. Even ardent Liverpudlians showed a grudging admiration for the big man's contributions and aerial prowess.

In April 1997, he earned a point at Goodison with a powerful drive which again left James picking the ball out of his net.

The following February, he scored at Anfield with another fine shot as the Blues earned a share of the spoils.

His fourth goal against the team across the park came in April 2001 when he fired home an equaliser in a dramatic game which saw the Blues edged out by the odd goal in five.

Even in playing a cameo role as a substitute in the Goodison win in December 2004, his delight at putting one over the Reds was plain for all to see.

His passion sometimes spilled over into the unsavoury - run-ins with Jason McAteer and Sami Hyypia will linger long in the memory - but he was never dismissed against the Blues' city rivals and played with the determination demanded by every Evertonian.

His delight at putting one over the Reds was plain for all to see - as shown by his celebrations following the 1-0 win at Goodison in December 2004 in which he had plated a cameo role as a late substitute.

Big Dunc

DUNCAN'S DERBY GOALS

21/11/94. Everton 2 (Ferguson, Rideout) Liverpool 0.

16/04/97. Everton 1 (Ferguson) Liverpool 1.

21/02/98. Liverpool 1 Everton 1 (Ferguson).

16/04/01. Everton 2 (Ferguson, Unsworth) Liverpool 3.

Dunc

ON EVERTON'S 1995 FA CUP FINAL VICTORY

"I'd never been to Wembley before and it certainly lived up to my expectations. I knew it would be an imposing stadium and obviously winning was the best feeling.

"We enjoyed ourselves and I'm sure all the fans did.

"I was nowhere near match fit and was lucky to even be on the bench. I was made up when the gaffer picked me. The lap of honour was good and someone out of the crowd threw me a blue nose.

"It was just a great day and I'd love to go back. It was a good night after the match and there were a few good speeches, including one from the gaffer.

"I had my kilt on. We let ourselves go, and why not?

"We were in a tricky position when I joined, but everyone knew if we worked hard the season wasn't necessarily over. To win the FA Cup in my first season was brilliant. I am very happy and don't want to move anywhere.

"They would have to drag me out of Goodison Park!"

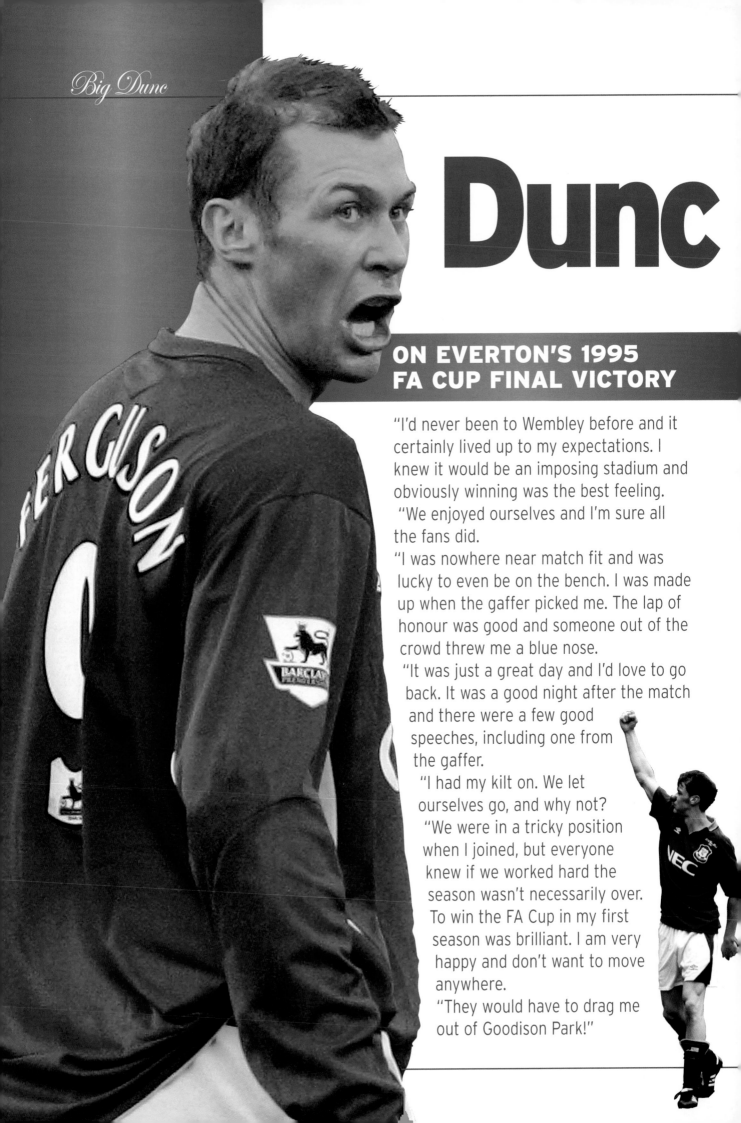

talking Blue

ON HIS GAME

" I have never been a big goalscorer, but I can get my fair share and help create them for others. I would love to get into the box and score, but sometimes when things are not going too well, you drop back and look for the ball. I feel comfortable on the ball just outside the area. I don't see myself as just a big target man "

ON AMOKACHI'S WEDDING!

"I went to Daniel Amokachi's wedding in Tunisia with a couple of mates for a few days and we had a great time. We were at the reception at a posh hotel and it was certainly an experience. It was good for somebody from the club to go. Daniel was made up when he saw me and very surprised. He just said he was glad I was there. He didn't know I was coming and it was a spur of the moment decision really. I just wanted to get away for a few days.

"Daniel had a bit of a rough time at the beginning of the 1994-95 season, but came through well at the end."

ON JOE ROYLE

"He has a good reputation both as a manager and as a player.

"They tell me he was a centre forward but that was a wee bit before my time!

"Seriously though, I have heard so much about him and obviously he was a quality player. I think he was hoping to take something from his Everton football days to his Everton manager days. I think he was made up that he could emulate that by helping us win the FA Cup."

ON THE FANS

"When I'm out and about in Liverpool I do get recognised, especially being so big and good looking! But the fans have been great to me.

"All this so-called 'Fergie mania' is unbelievable. What can I say? They have been treated to a good tradition of watching their number nines, so if I can live up to some of their expectations I'll be more than happy.

"You cannot help but have a good feeling for Everton. I want to do well for the team. The tremendous support that we get just shows the potential of the club.

"And any charity work which I do is just to try to put a wee bit back."

Other than The Queen, Duncan is probably Britain's most famous pigeon fancier. His hobby may be a little unusual but it was an interest he developed from an early age.

Speaking to The Evertonian magazine in April, 1995, he revealed: "I have had plenty of room-mates on away trips. They keep on swapping ... perhaps that's because I have been cooing in my sleep. I don't snore, I coo!

"I love my pigeons. Me and my dad started it together at home in Scotland and I really do love it.

"Everybody's got an interest outside their work and mine is just to race pigeons."

'I have had plenty of room-mates on away trips. They keep on swapping ... perhaps that's because I have been cooing in my sleep. I don't snore, I coo! I love my pigeons'

A heart of gold

DUNCAN cared about Everton and for him, that meant looking after the fans. Here's just a handful of pictures from the hundreds over the years that sum up the caring side of a Goodison giant . . .

DUNCAN never makes a song and dance about it - or courts publicity - but he has always been a keen supporter of local charities.

A good deal of his good work goes unreported and Joe Royle admitted the big man was one of the most generous

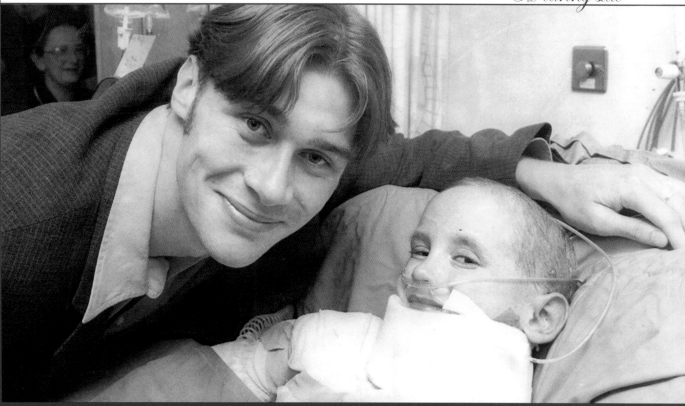

people he has encountered.

He would regularly take time out to visit sick children and was a massive hit with the club's young Academy players during the annual training days at Bellefield.

In issue five of The Evertonian, Duncan explained how he was hoping to raise £10,000 for Alder Hey by presenting fans with signed prints at £10 each.

"Any work which I do is just to try and put a wee bit back into the community and show the fans that I really do appreciate them," he said.

Every Christmas and Easter, Duncan has been a popular figure among the club visits to Alder Hey and Claire House but he carries out charity work year-long and deserves enormous credit for the support he has given to many worthy causes.

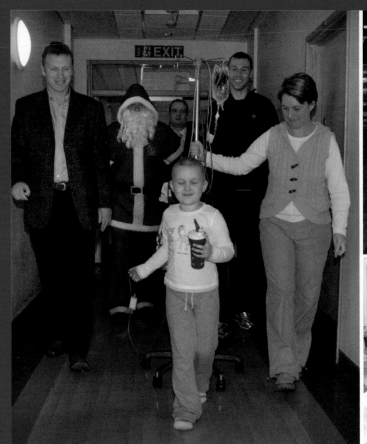

FROM a man mountain on the pitch to a gentle giant off it, Duncan left a lasting impression on many people in and around the world of football. Here's a few of the tributes he's been paid . . .

"Duncan Ferguson at his best week-in, week-out would have been in my team ahead of Ronaldo.

"That boy (Ronaldo) plays when the sun is shining. When you are ankle deep in mud you don't see Ronaldo.

"But you see Duncan hail, rain or snow - he just doesn't do it consistently enough."
TOMMY DOCHERTY

"Everton have always had great centre-forwards, starting with Dixie Dean. Then me, Alex Young, Andy Gray and now the young boy Duncan Ferguson.

"He could be one of the greatest the club has ever had. He is such a big lad that he hardly needs to jump for the ball and he has such a good touch for his height.

"His balance and positional play also make him a good player. If he looks after himself, he has the ability to be equally as good as Dixie Dean and I really mean that."
TOMMY LAWTON
(Speaking in 1998)

"He was world class - the only world class player Scotland had at that time."
WILLIE DONACHIE

"In the first 25 minutes, I thought we had a chance of pulling off a shock, but then Everton got their first goal. It was a great education for us and big Duncan was like a man mountain. He was magnificent and I don't think he gave the ball away once all night."
JOHN HOLLINS
(September 2003)

'People say he has a bad boy image. But they don't know him'

"People might say Duncan has this bad boy image which they keep reading about in the papers. But they don't know the lad.

"Duncan has an aversion to the Press, which is fair enough because he's had such a bad ride off them.

"With the greatest of respect, a lot of what is said about Duncan in the papers is clap-trap."

Parrott added that he had seldom seen anyone as proud as Ferguson when he was first handed the captain's armband. He responded with a hat-trick in a 3-2 defeat of Bolton.

"Quite honestly he was so proud to be captain that I kept saluting him when I saw him. I would have left him as captain. Anyone who gets his arm tattooed with an Everton emblem and the number nine on it for the rest of his life is serious about the club he plays for.

"Talking to him he was so proud to wear the armband running out on that pitch, you wouldn't believe it.

"I'm delighted he scored his hat-trick against Bolton because for far too long he's been playing in a team where he hasn't been getting particularly good service.

"Duncan will score goals like that and would definitely be in double figures if Everton had a recognised winger who could cross the ball."

JOHN PARROTT
(Speaking to The Evertonian in February 1998 about his brother-in-law)

"The people who criticised the club for that didn't know what Duncan meant to the fans. He was the right man at the right time for us. He roused the passion at Goodison. He is a supporters' player. He knew what we wanted and we knew what he could give us."

JIM KING (of the Everton Supporters Club, in February 2000, on the reaction to Joe Royle visiting Ferguson in prison and the celebrations when the player emerged from the tunnel at Goodison to run out for his first match, piped onto the field and feted by the crowd. King was also in The Winslow pub opposite Goodison Park the night Ferguson was sold to Newcastle in November 1998 and he remembers Ferguson's father coming in to thank the supporters for the reception they had given his son).

"Put it this way, I'd rather be playing with him than against him."

ALAN SHEARER
(Ex-Newcastle team-mate)

"When I first came to the club, people were saying to me 'God help you with Duncan, he is always injured', so I was a bit reticent you know, but I can honestly say that every injury he has had has been a genuine one and he has got the scars to prove it.

"It might be interesting to note that since last March, when he recovered from that big operation on the nerve that was trapped in his buttock, I don't think he has missed a day's training apart from when he was quite ill and was a couple of weeks away.

"There was also of course that little problem with the manager when Duncan was away from the training ground for a bit but otherwise he has been training every day.

"It will surprise a lot of people I know when I say that Duncan comes in here every Sunday on his own to do his own training and on regular training days he is often first in and the last to leave."

MICK RATHBONE (2004)
(Everton Physio)

"He would be the last person on earth to get involved in anything like this. Maybe the person concerned has just misheard whatever has been said."

DANIEL AMOKACHI (Regarding a race row with Fulham striker Luis Boa Morte, alleged to have taken place in February 2004)

"Duncan has got quite a few important goals for us this season, coming on as substitute in particular. Now it's been two in a week for us and they were both big goals. On his day he is unplayable, and we are seeing him at his very best at the moment, he doesn't seem to lose a header out there."
NIGEL MARTYN (April 2005)

"I don't think Jaap Stam enjoyed playing against him because he gave him a torrid time. He fought him in the air, he fought him on the touchline. I think Stam probably found Ferguson the toughest, most awkward striker he has played against this season - including the Champions League.
  "Scotland could do with him, you haven't got anybody up there like him.
  "Hey, we haven't got anybody down here like him. Kevin Phillips is not like him, Andy Cole is not like him, Teddy Sheringham is not like him.
  "You could do with him and you might have a chance because he's beginning to love the industry he's working in now, he's more in love with it."
SIR BOBBY ROBSON
(In February 2000)

"I noticed when he came on and had a good look at him. He's not moving that much. He's not a man running 10 metres here and 10 metres there. He's just waiting for the right moment and it came. Scoring goals is what he's paid for and he might be clever just to show up in the box when it matters. If people say he's an old fashioned player, fine, but I would say that's a fashion that is never out of style!"
THOMAS HELVEG (October 2004)

"Duncan is a true pro. When he isn't playing, he is always in on his days off and when he is playing he has real presence. People say he has a wild side, but I wouldn't change one bit of him. That's what makes him Duncan Ferguson, he is a great player to play with and has shown how he is worth his weight in gold. You saw Birmingham took a step back when he came on. That's his presence. He affects defenders mentally and he is in a rich vein of form and we have to try and exploit that and get as much out of it as we can".
TIM CAHILL (April 2005)

"I hear Big Fergie likes a few pints, loves to stay out late and chase the birds and gives a bit of lip in training; in my book he has all the ingredients of a good footballer."
JIM BAXTER

"I used to pick Duncan up for training and he would give me lifts too, so I probably know him as well as anyone. He is just a lad with a heart of gold. I like Duncan a lot and I think he has been unfortunate in the way things have happened to him. There are certainly worse characters in the game."
GARY STEVENS
(Former Glasgow Rangers team-mate)

"I first saw Duncan as a 15-year-old when he was playing in trials for Scotland Under-16s. My son Jason was in the same team before he picked up a serious injury.

"I remember Duncan was big and gangly and very thin. He didn't do a lot of heading and the main thing I noticed was that he had a nice touch on his left foot."
ALEX YOUNG

"You can talk all you want about him. Everton was built on a man like Duncan Ferguson, a personality like that right back to Dixie Dean. And we have built British football on characters like this."
BOBBY GOULD (Ex-Wales manager)

"Some people seem to regard him as not much more than a targetman, a good one mind you. But there is a lot more to Duncan than that. Besides being so dangerous in the air, he is great at ground level. He has a very sure touch for a big man and is unbelievably difficult to shake off the ball. He has got everything."
GARY McALLISTER
(Former Scotland team-mate)

"Everybody knows that Duncan's record against Manchester United is excellent. He didn't stop running all night, which maybe disproved a couple of things. He showed great energy and he showed that he's a big time player for the big occasion. There's not many people with his record. He took his goal really well. I've got to say that it was an excellent delivery from Mikel Arteta that gave Duncan a chance to finish it off. He's had a great record but more important than his goal for me was how hard he worked. His all round team play was as good as I've seen from Duncan for a long time."
DAVID MOYES (April 2005)

"I first saw Duncan as a youth player with Dundee United and he was an outstanding talent even then. He had great ability for a big fella, but strangely enough it wasn't his aerial power which first caught my eye.

"He had excellent close control and a good footballing touch for such a big man and it was that part of his game which most impressed me."
CRAIG BROWN
(Former Scotland manager)

"Big Dunc's a bit of an enigma really. I've been told what he does off the pitch and you've got to hold your hands up and say; 'Terrific guy.' But I question whether he's going to be satisfied with what he's done on the pitch with his career as opposed to what he does off the pitch.

"For a man who has got everything that you'd want in a centre-forward, I'm not sure. He might be one of those players who thinks: 'Fine, yes, I've had a good career, I'm happy with it,' but it just seems he could have given more and done more and played for Scotland more and whatever.

"Sometimes you just think: 'Oh Dunc, you can do it, you can do it'.

"I don't know. But when he plays and he's playing well and he wants to play, there's no-one better.

"Maybe history will suggest he could have done more but he may be content with what he's done, so you'd have to ask him. Other people may think: 'Dear me, he could have done more' and so on, but he may think he's done as much as he could do. And if he says that, you've got to respect that. He's certainly had everything a centre-forward needs... I wouldn't want to have played against him as an opposing centre-half."
BOB LATCHFORD

'Dunc was my talisman'

"There was too much paper talk about Duncan signing for us and that's why it seemed to drag on a bit.

"Instead of being able to turn around to the supporters and say: 'This is Duncan Ferguson, we have signed him,' everybody was already expecting it and waiting for it because of the media coverage.

"In terms of actual figures, the £4m deal which brought Duncan to Goodison was probably as much as I spent in 12 years as Oldham manager.

"We had seen Duncan at close range and we knew there was a shortage of top class strikers. He had the

– Joe Royle

potential to be one of the biggest and one of the best.

"Duncan was never a problem to me. He is a lovely big man.

"The only fight you'd get involved in with Duncan was when there was a charity raffle and you'd have to fight him to buy something because he was so generous.

"He was terrific for me - the talisman in the recovery in 1994-95."

'The only fight you'd get involved in with Duncan was when there was a charity raffle and you'd have to fight him to buy something because he was so generous'

A Dunc date . . .

In 1996, The Evertonian ran a special competition to win a date with Duncan!

Anna Reece was the winner of the competition which attracted a huge response.

Anna's day to remember began with a tour of the Blues' Bellefield training ground, before Duncan drove her for a meal at a Liverpool restaurant. The teenager was joined on the day out by her grandmother Dolly, who nominated Anna after she had overcome a serious illness to take up a place at Manchester University, studying French and German.

Anna said afterwards: "I had a brilliant day and I think my Gran was more nervous than me when we were driving to Bellefield.

"The best part of the day was being driven to Bellefield in Duncan's car. He was really friendly and down to earth. Just as I expected."

'The best part of the day was being driven to Bellefield in Duncan's car. He was really friendly and down to earth. Just as I expected'

Season	League		Cup		Total	
	Apps	**Gls**	**Apps**	**Gls**	**Apps**	**Gls**
1994/95	22(1)	7	4(1)	1	26(2)	8
1995/96	16(2)	5	2(0)	2	18(2)	7
1996/97	31(2)	10	3(0)	1	34(2)	11
1997/98	28(1)	11	3(0)	0	31(1)	11
1998/99	13(0)	4	4(0)	1	17	5
2000/01	9(3)	6	1(0)	0	10(3)	6
2001/02	17(5)	6	3(0)	2	20(5)	8
2002/03	0(7)	0	0(1)	0	0(8)	0
2003/04	13(7)	5	4(0)	4	17(7)	9
2004/05	6(29)	5	2(0)	1	8(29)	6
2005/06	7(20)	1	3(3)	0	10(23)	1
Overall	**162(77)**	**60**	**29(5)**	**12**	**191(82)**	**72**

The People's verdict

WHEN icLiverpool asked Blues fans to leave their tributes to Dunc on their website messageboard, they were flooded with replies. Here's a selection of your views on the big man . . .

'The man is a legend and in two seasons he kept us up single-handedly. The amount of passion he shows for the club is immense. I hope he will return as a coach, because the youngsters could learn a lot from him. All the best big man.'
Andrei from Liverpool

'Big Dunc is a true Blue and a legend on the Gwladys Street End. As for his playing ability, he hasn't always produced the goals but you can see he is a true Evertonian - just look at the tattoo.'
Ian from Liverpool

'Duncan is an absolute hero. Apart from the odd fight which has let us down, Duncan is in the same league as a legend. With the service he has given to this club, he deserved a real send-off on the last day off the season'
Phil Gray from Pocklington

'Duncan is undoubtedly a legend. Yes he has his faults, and he's let us down on occasions, but he's given us some great times, and the effect he has on the crowd will never be matched. We'll never forget you.'
James from Liverpool

'I hope he can have a testimonial. Sure he has got into trouble too many times for some. But you cannot fault his loyalty and his love for EFC. The Manchester United match last season saw him at his old unplayable best against the best. Thanks big Dunc.'
Phil Chappell from Woodside

'Duncan has been and will always be my hero. As a relatively young Evertonian at 15 I haven't seen many greats but this man has touched my heart and he will always be a legend to me, no doubt.'
Joe Jennings from Liverpool

'I have been a disciple of big Dunc ever since he arrived, and particularly after that first goal against Liverpool. His genuine love of the club, never-say-die attitude, natural ability, and occasional acts of recklessness, make him a one-off enigma, and all-time Goodison hero. I have loved each and every one of his goals, but my personal favourite was when he turned on the edge of the box and curled the ball around David James into the bottom corner at the Gwladys Street End in 1997. He has always done things for charity, and cared about the fans that idolise him. Last year he was good enough to send a congratulations and best wishes letter to me and my wife on our wedding day, after a friend had contacted him. A surreal moment when it was read out by my best man, but magical. Duncan Ferguson, an Everton legend, without a doubt.'
Mark McDermott from Oxford

'Dunc is a legend, not a prolific goalscorer but what he does for a team is remarkable. The pride, passion and aggression he provides for the team is second-to-none. He makes other teams scared to play Everton. A 6ft 4" big man that has a blue heart.'
'JJ'

'Once a Blue always a Blue. I wonder where we have heard that before! Only this time you know it's right. He may have had his moments but give me 11 Duncan Fergusons and I'll give you a top-five finish every time.'
Keith Baxendale from Buckley, North Wales

'Duncan Ferguson was a hero when we needed one. On his day he was one of the best forwards the Premiership has seen. And a true gentleman. Oh, and he won more trophies with Everton than Shearer did for Newcastle!'
Kev from Liverpool

'The Everton number nine shirt is one of the most significant in the league. Duncan Ferguson can quite rightly wear that shirt with pride. I for one think the man has brought hope to our club in some very troubled times - he fought (both with fists and feet!) for Everton and us fans in every game he played. Have a happy future big man.'
Mike Trueman

'The man has been the sole reason for about 10 seasons (give or take a couple when he left) why Everton fans get excited about watching Everton, whether he's going in for challenges, leading the team as our inspirational captain or scoring important goals, thanks for being our hero Dunc.'
Paul Mitty from Liverpool

'Duncan is a hero and my best memory is when he was released from prison and came on the pitch at the home game against Sheffield Wednesday (while he was still banned by the Scottish FA). Nobody knew he was going to make an appearance before the game and Goodison went absolutely beserk - the whole ground was singing his name - even people in the directors' box! The Wednesday fans were stunned because they went 2-0 up and we were all still singing for Duncan (the game finished 2-2). He has been my hero since I was 14 and I am 26 now and Everton won't feel the same without him, he has been a part of my Everton and he is a legend!'
Jon Sullivan from Wallasey

'Ferguson stands for everything that is Everton FC - working class and one of the people.'
'Moosetalks' from London

'When we were at rock bottom in 1994 Joe Royle came and big Dunc followed his lead. The two of them lifted us and I will never forget that season. I know we won the FA Cup final but every match from Joe taking over with Duncan in the side was like a cup final. Goals against Liverpool and Manchester United that season made him a hero. Being sold behind his back to Newcastle by Peter Johnson in a sense made him even more of a legend. What a fellow!'
Terry Turner from Chorley

Big Dunc always has been - and always will be - a True Blue. I'll miss you and your attitude, football is a contact sport! Good luck lad!
Patrick from Montego Bay

Big Dunc

'I'll be heartbroken when Duncan goes. He is a superb footballer who suffered for want of good striking partners. Critics of his injury record forget he played with an injury for a whole season and kept us up in 1998. He suffers because of a Press determined to make him pay for not speaking to them. He doesn't need to talk to them, he talks to us. Real fans know he carried the club for years, giving us pride when we had nothing, the player we look to when the chips are down. His disciplinary record is poor, but how many times has he been punished because of who he is? How many times is he kicked and the referee takes no action? I've lost count of the times I've heard Blues say they want Dunc to smack players, then criticise him for doing just that. Duncan isn't perfect, but he's been a genuine hero for this club, we will never see his like again. Thanks Duncan, you will never be forgotten.'
Gaynor Ford from Liverpool

'One of the greatest Everton players ever! He has earned his place in Everton's hall of fame! He's a living legend!'
Harri from Lohja, Finland

'A legend, a dying breed, and if not for his injury problems, could have been one of the best strikers in the world let alone Premiership. His feet are as good as his head, and his lack of pace is made up for in his passion, pride and determination. I'll miss you Dunc.'
Charlie from North Wales

'Let me say this, any charity in the world would be lucky to have Duncan working for them for £30,000 a week. But he does it for nothing. Yes he has been one of our highest-paid players ever, but the goals he has scored have kept the club in the Premier League. And get this! How many players have their team's badge tattooed on their arms? Thank you Duncan for the good times and for giving us back some of our pride.'
Richy Styles from Everton

DUNCAN'S FAREWELL MESSAGE TO THE FANS

"I would like to express my heartfelt gratitude to all the Everton fans for the wonderful reception I received at the West Brom game.

"On Sunday at the end of the game the emotion I felt at seeing my family sharing that famous Goodison experience with me was overwhelming. It was a moment of pure magic that I shall never ever forget.

"Throughout my career at Everton I have experienced a wonderful feeling of being accepted by the fans as 'one of the family' and the friendliness extended to me by all Liverpool people over the past 10 years has been fantastic. Whilst the Liverpool sense of humour is known throughout the world, for me the city's greatest asset is the friendliness of the people.

"I would like to believe that the passion that I have for Everton is the equal to that of all the magnificent fans."

**Duncan Ferguson,
May 2006**

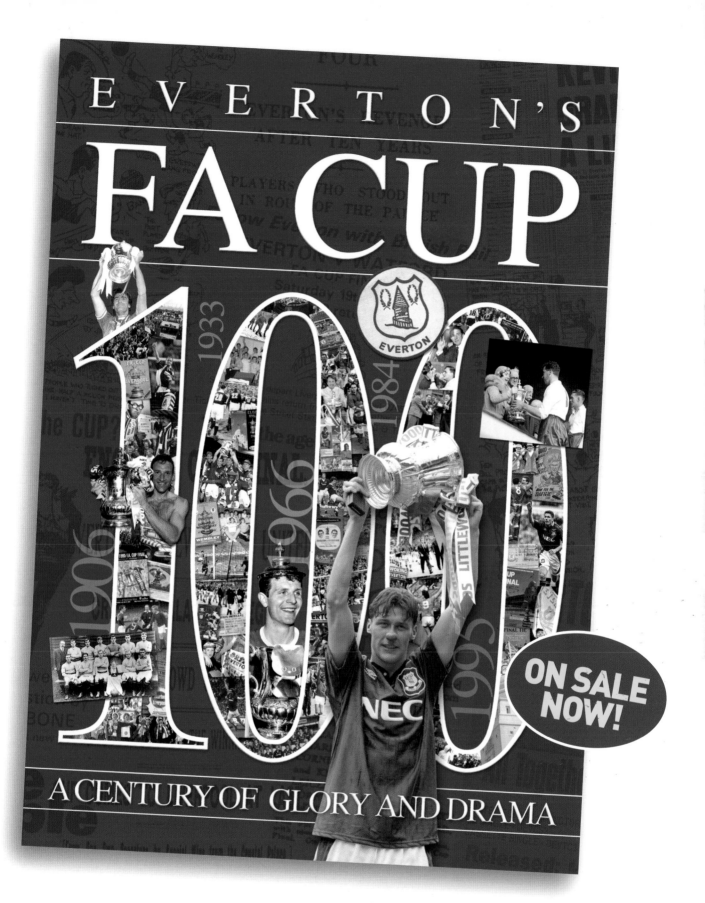

EVERTON'S

FA CUP 100

A CENTURY OF GLORY AND DRAMA

ON SALE NOW!

'I will never, ever forget the Everton fans.

The support I have received from the people of Liverpool is special.

Everton fans are part of my blood because of the way they have

stood by me. Their loyalty to me is one of the main reasons why

I love Everton so much'

ISBN 1905266189

9 781905 266180